NORTHERN KENT

Edited by Lucy Jenkins

First published in Great Britain in 1999 by
YOUNG WRITERS
Remus House,
Coltsfoot Drive,
Woodston,
Peterborough, PE2 9JX
Telephone (01733) 890066

HB ISBN 0 75431 670 X
SB ISBN 0 75431 671 8

FOREWORD

Young Writers have produced poetry books in conjunction with schools for over eight years; providing a platform for talented young people to shine. This year, the Celebration 2000 collection of regional anthologies were developed with the millennium in mind.

With the nation taking stock of how far we have come, and reflecting on what we want to achieve in the future, our anthologies give a vivid insight into the thoughts and experiences of the younger generation.

We were once again impressed with the quality and attention to detail of every entry received and hope you will enjoy the poems we have decided to feature in *Celebration 2000 Northern Kent* for many years to come.

CONTENTS

Joy Lane Junior School

	Amy Lucy	54
	Joseph Masters	54
	Daniel Lamba	55
	Lucy Gustafson	55
	Ben Croucher	56
	Freyja Ambler	56
	Billy McNamara	57
	Simon Fosbraey	57
	Christopher Edwards	58
	Adam Davidge	58
	Sarah Gilbert	59
	James Blakebrough	60
	David Humphreys	61
	Nicola Cox	62

Junior King's School

	Gabriella Coombe	62
	Alex Sanné	63
	Olivia Byrne	63
	Joshua Maley	64
	William Bruce	64
	Anna Broxup	65
	Poppy Mitchell	65
	Joanna Brilliant	66
	Timothy Leung	66
	Joshua Blinston Jones	67
	James Lynes	68
	Elsa Butrous	68
	Philip Spicer	69
	Craig Anthony Sawyer	70
	Olenka Hamilton	71
	Harry Lancaster	72

Northdown CP School

	Callum Costa	72
	Roxanne Trent	73
	James Steven Brown	73
	Ty Fairbrother	74

Paul Hodges	75
David Wraight	75
Marianne Hollins	76
Becky Elks	76
Katie Burke	77
Alan Bennett	78
Amanda Wellard	78
Lianne Ramshaw	79
Cara Downer	79
Ashley Knight	80
Maria Adkins	80
Edward Ayres	81
Jemma Hills	81
Kayleigh Hammond	81
Jodi Bovington	82
Samantha Buttigieg	82
Kyle Easton	82
Lee Fairbrother	83
Kayleigh Ward	83

Parkwood Junior School

Lee Ludlow	83
Amy Millbank	84
Natalie Filmer	85
Roxanne Ianson	86
Ian Chambers & Nicholas Long	87
Thomas Ball	88
Rebecca Heale	89
Jade Caccavone	90
Simon Lucas	91
Charlene Cotter	92
Alex Forster	93
Rhys Mant	94
Stacey Meaney	95
Kizzy Ripley	96
Anouska Lafferty & Lenna Rogers	97
Levi Courtney & Holly Preston	98
Zoe Porter	98

St Benedict's RC Primary School, Chatham

Zoe Etheridge	120
Karen Gordon	121
Jemma Collins	121
Peter Vik	122
Luke Thorne	122
Michelle Barton	123
Gary Crawford	124
Martin McDaid	124
Anneliese Clare D'Souza	125
Leanne Ferguson	125
Amy Caulfield	126
Lauren Parsons	126
Oliver Robert Barnard	127
Laura Simpson	127
Jason Gary Evatt	128

St Botolph's CEP School, Northfleet

Emma Parrick	128
Mark Blowers	129
Charlotte Parks	129
Dominic Barnes	130
Katy Heasman	130
Bradley Jarrett	131
Hannah Siggers	132
Leslie Barrass	132
Jodi Laura Parmenter	133
Jennifer Moule	133
Daniel Dadwal	134
Krystal Burton-Grey	134
Kerry Reilly	135
Kevin Parrick	135
Katie Archer	136
Anna Chan	136
Stephen Bage	137
Louise Fielder-White	137
Kayleigh-Anne Soryal	138
Hannah Payne	138

Carlie Warren	139
Rebecca Hall	139
Laura Chan	140
Jason Bright	140
Zoe Blowers	141
Philip Beech	141
Jamie Davies	142
Aran Wade	142
Carly Dickman	143
Clare Oliver	143
James Willis	144
Kallie M Heap	144
Christine Martin	145
James Payne	145
Tarren Sharp	145
Ross Maynard	146
Shirell Spicer	146
Tony Barham	146

St Helen's CE Primary School, Cliffe

Sam Isaacs	147
Megan Jeffrey	147
Sarah Ebbs	148
Dean Ellis	148
Samantha Louise Mitchell	149
Hannah Loveridge	149
Lewis Rixson	150
Kayleigh Herbert	150
Maxine Shaw	151
Ashleigh Ahkin	151
Jessica Springhall	152
Ben Blackman	152
Hollie Slater	153
Lauren Medcraft	153
Alex Turner	154
Lucy Henrick	154
Maria Richards	155
Oliver Theobald	155

Michael Baxendale	195
Katie Bosley	195
Kimberley Murphy	196
Andrew Steven Wright	196
Timothy Reynolds	197
Anthony Kay	197
Gemma Glover	198
James Stuart	198
Martyn James Jarrett	199
Mikaela Jade Simmers	199
Joanna Oakley	200
Melanie Laver	200
Ben Conway	201
Jonathan Ward	201
Charlene Lucy Kay	201
Jordon Pritchett	202

Thames View Junior School

Jonathon Stewart	202
Lauren Coombes	203
Alex Allen	203
Hayley Chapman	204
Carl Temple	204
Charlotte Knight	205
Aneesha Tiwari	205
Samuel Jordan	206
Hannah Baker	206
Faye Andrew	206
Paul More & Aaron Bass	207
Roxanne Hemans-Davis	207
Megan Wright	208
Clark Taylor	208
Hannah Ayres	209
Katy Everett	210
Carla Stepney	210
Stephanie Cordes	211
Robert Davies	212
Rebecca Stone	212

The Poems

FOX

Prowling round the forest floor
Its favourite prey is no more.
Shiny red coat and pure black socks
As it leaps between the rocks.

See him run,
Oh see him run,
Lighter than the wind
And smoother than the sun.

Watch him eating his lunch,
Gobble, gobble, munch, munch.
Running round the forest free,
Keeping away from you and me.

See him run,
Oh see him run,
Lighter than the wind
And smoother than the sun.

Joy Blake (9)
Barrow Grove Junior School

TEACHER'S PET

Teacher's pet isn't a boy or a girl
Teacher's pet isn't brainy
Teacher's pet is missing
Teacher is hunting for his pet
Crawling around and calling his name
'Bruce!' he calls, 'Bruce! Bruce! Bruce!'
Teacher's pet is a great big tarantula.

Karl Ticehurst (10)
Barrow Grove Junior School

THE MILLENNIUM

The year two thousand will be grand,
It will bring lots of news, good or bad.
There will be lots of pictures of the Millennium Dome.
In the new decade we will be strong,
We will forgive those who have done wrong.

Jason Fathers (10)
Barrow Grove Junior School

THE YEAR TWO THOUSAND

The year two thousand is a year of celebrations.
Wish and wish - your wishes might come true.
The year two thousand is what you really need.
Just dance and dance all night
You can celebrate the year
2000.

Aimee Manester (7)
Barrow Grove Junior School

SUMMER

Summer makes the sky so blue
as the fledgling birds hatch from a tree.
Not a cloud in sight, just the smell
of buttercups and poppies.
A bee goes buzzing by to suck
the nectar out of a flower.

Avril Jarrett (8)
Barrow Grove Junior School

GOING SWIMMING

Going swimming
in the cold, cold, water.
People splashing around,
people getting very, very, wet and cold.
The look on your face is terrible
when you're underwater.
The water gets in your mouth,
and up your nose.
The smell of the water is disgusting,
but swimming is really, really, *great.*

Kirsty Bell (10)
Barrow Grove Junior School

MILLENNIUM

I wish the millennium would hurry up and come,
I think that it will be great fun!
Families will be together, smiling happy as can be,
I've asked my mum for a big present,
but she only says, 'I'll see!'
My friends will have a party and everyone will be there,
singing, dancing, having a good time.
I hope it's never-ending and goes on like a circle.
So I guess I'll have to wait, be patient,
and maybe I'll get a present.
Well, I'll have to go now, I'm going to mark the
days off my calendar.

Emily Luxton (10)
Delce Junior School

CHRISTMAS DAY 1914

(This poem is about the Christmas truce in 1914, when British and German soldiers emerged from their trenches and exchanged food and drink, played football and sang carols. No more shots were heard for all of Christmas Day)

We waited in the darkness
Breathing musty air,
Our hands were cold and clammy,
And our hearts were full of fear.

'No Man's Land' was still,
No noise, no shouts, no shots, no death,
Just an eerie silence all around.

Suddenly, we heard a sweet, sad tune.
One that we all knew,
The beautiful song of 'Silent Night'
Drifted across the field,
German voices quiet and soft,
We heard loud and clear.

I joined my fellow soldiers as they sang,
Our voices trembling in shock.
We threw our guns back into the trench,
And marched to 'No Man's Land'.

There we united
With the German men.
We joked and kicked a football.
Smiles and laughter reigned.

No, I'll never forget that Christmas Day in 1914,
When British and Germans alike
Found room for peace in 'No Man's Land'.

Abigail Tucker (11)
Delce Junior School

TIME

Time's like a path
we walk down every day.
It's with us when we breathe,
when we talk and with the words we say.
Time's like a heart,
pumping out all our life,
time can cause tension,
like a rolling dice.
We all think we've got too much time to spare,
but every tick of that clock
is giving us another chance to make peace,
and care.
As the millennium falls ever nearer,
day by day,
we celebrate time, as a symbol
of how we've lived our lives,
in so many different ways.

Jessica Gearey (11)
Delce Junior School

WE COULD NOT DO WITHOUT IT

Television, television!
No one, nothing, can take it away.
Washing machine, washing machine!
Persil, Ariel and Vanish,
Asda, Tesco and Safeways.
What would we do without them?
PlayStations, Segas and Gameboys,
I could not live without them.

Nicholas Wright (11)
Delce Junior School

MILLENNIUM

Millennium, millennium,
Millennium, millennium,
First man on the moon,
Millennium, millennium,
Someone invented literacy hour.
Millennium, millennium,
Someone invented computers.
Millennium, millennium,
The First World War.
Millennium, millennium,
Second World War.
Millennium, millennium,
Caves were found.
Millennium, millennium,
Little and big Furbys were invented.
Millennium, millennium,
A different way of life,
Millennium, millennium,
Millennium, millennium.

Charlotta Watson (8)
Delce Junior School

MR WIND

If I climb to the top of a mountain,
I would find him there.
He would be inside a wood,
For he is everywhere.

He whistles and whirls,
But loves to play.
He dances and sings
All through the day.

His song so cheerful,
His caper so sweet
He gracefully moves
Those breezy feet.

A leaf of card
To a wall is pinned,
All because of
That Mr Wind.

Craig Beadle (9)
Delce Junior School

MILLENNIUM BUG

The Millennium Bug is nothing but a slug,
it is very slow, but on the go.
Trouble is, it's game and fame is its name.
It will go down in the history books with Tony Blair,
I think they'd make quite a pair!

The Millennium Bug is nothing but a slug,
it has people running here and there,
getting twists in their underwear.
We have computers that are going to break down,
and if they did, Tony Blair would look quite a clown!

The Millennium Bug is nothing but a slug,
it makes all our lives hell,
who knows what will happen, who can tell?
Take it as it comes, that's how I look at it,
if your computer does break down,
just throw a book at it!

Gemma Simon (10)
Delce Junior School

A New Millennium, A New World

Adults will be very small
And children very tall.
Blackboards will be red,
There'll be people with no heads.
All girls will play football
And boys will wear dresses,
Men will do the housework
And women make the messes.
Teachers will be dumb
And children very smart,
We'll be good at maths,
And the teachers good at art.
We won't have a lot of money,
We won't have a lot to eat,
We'll live on fruit and honey,
And won't have any feet.

Kerri Bunce (9)
Delce Junior School

Celebration

Good luck.
Celebration
For the millennium.
Celebration
For everyone.
Celebration,
Everyone's happy.
I don't want it to end.
Celebration.

Jeevan Dhesy (8)
Delce Junior School

PAST AND PRESENT TIMES

In the year 1900,
Life was not like it is now.
Things have changed an awful lot,
So sit back, and let me tell you how.

Computers, PlayStations, TVs
Were not invented then,
So take a moment to think
How lucky we are to have them.

People made their own entertainment,
Dancing, plays or singing.
There was no electricity
Or a telephone to keep on ringing.

Now, electricity is one of the things
Of modern, every day life.
We have TVs, radios,
And a handy, electric knife.

The care is one of the things
That people use every day.
This takes them from place to place,
But people still say:

'I've got to do the shopping,
Pick the children up from school,
Fetch Auntie Doris from the hospital,
Go and buy Granny a footstool.'

If you are one of these people,
Ungrateful for what you've got,
Read back through this poem
And think about it and awful lot.

Laura Trussell (11)
Delce Junior School

THE WHALE

There is a ripple in the water,
A spurt from the depths below,
Never in order, but in time
Don't fear, we hear your calls.

The face of nature's beauty
Rising from the sunset sea beyond,
As he greets the dawning dusk,
The memory to be belonged.

As he disappears into an echoing home,
Where his family wait for him hearing his blessing cries,
Returning to his heaven, disappearing into the blue,
He looks at me through his ever-powerful eyes.

He was now just a picture I never would see,
But a ripple in the water, could it be true,
Or was it just me,
Or my daydream mind had the inevitable come true?

A head appeared from the water
As gentle as before, but with a faint smile,
Never dare not to go faster,
His shadow the spirit of the water.

Now rising higher than ever before
His great tail lashes at the water,
Exactly like an eagle
Over the water he seems to soar.

Into the water he plunges,
His tail waves goodbye.
I'm free, let's keep it that way,
He seemed to reply.

This sight I never will see again,
Gone from the eyes that slay his kind,
he's free and that's most important to me.
Goodbye, my gentle giant.

The face of nature's beauty,
Rising from the sunset sea beyond
As he greets the dawning dusk
The memory to me belonged.

Lauren Heritage (10)
Delce Junior School

ANOTHER YEAR OVER

December the 31st again,
Oh what a wonderful day.
December the 31st again,
A new year on its way.
Another day until the new year,
Another nearly over.
Another day until the new year,
And it will start all over.
But this year it is special,
It will be the millennium.
Another thousand years have gone by,
I wonder what will happen?
Should everything just be the same, or
Should it all be different?
But for all I know, it's another year,
Just like any other.

Hayley Gallagher (10)
Delce Junior School

CHOCOLATE!

There is a countdown for the
Year 2000, from Mars,
So all the chocolate bars will be ours!

Buttons float through the sky,
Bags of Bounties fly.
Chocolate, chocolate, chocolate.

Galaxy dreams through space,
Streams of Cadbury flow at their own pace.
Chocolate, chocolate, chocolate.

Cadbury's Creme Eggs
Roll round Saturn's ring,
While Smarties go plop and ping.
Chocolate, chocolate, chocolate.

Mars bars, chocolate bars,
Milky Way, Galaxy,
Take their position
In the countdown for the year!

Adrianne Paige (10)
Delce Junior School

DREAMING

Floating in the world of dreams,
Flying over where the stars beam.
No one wants to wake up
From the world of dreams.

Hannah Edwards (10)
Delce Junior School

RAIN, CLOUDS AND RIVER

Raindrops make things beautiful,
The grass and flowers too.
If raindrops make things beautiful,
Why doesn't it rain on you?

The river is deep, I look at the
Clouds and I fall asleep.
The clouds are so pretty, they fade away.
Oh, what a beautiful day.

The river is coming,
It is heading our way,
And now it's gone,
Hip, hip, hooray.

Hayleigh Salt (9)
Delce Junior School

GOALKEEPERS

Goalkeepers, goalkeepers, diving about,
Goalkeepers, goalkeepers always giving a shout.
Goalkeepers, goal keepers with rock solid hands,
How can Bartez even stand?
Goalkeepers, goalkeepers with such a kick,
Goalkeepers, goalkeepers I wish they wouldn't spit.
Goalkeepers, goalkeepers saving loads of shots,
Goalkeepers, goalkeepers they don't go around in yachts.
Goalkeepers, goalkeepers losing, winning, drawing,
A goalkeeper's job isn't very boring.
Goalkeepers, goalkeepers sometimes let the team down,
More often than not, they wear the crown.

Sam Stratford (8)
Grove Park School

MY MAGIC BOX

My box is made of dragon's scales
Made into a patchwork blanket and
A teapot's jumper.

Its hinges are flies' legs.
It's lined with the fabric of time
And treasures found at the end of the rainbow.

Inside my box, I keep a twinkling star
From the midnight sky,
And a Dodo's egg, along with a phoenix's feather.

I hide my box inside a clock's face,
Smiling like a clown.

Jason Cesary (11)
Grove Park School

MY MAGIC BOX

My box is made of a feather of the mountains
and the cry of the sky.
Its hinges are made of the skin of a skeleton.
It is lined with the piece of sky that broke my heart,
and the wind in my mind.
Inside my box, I keep the light of my soul
and the floating sound of a waterfall.
I hide my box in the mouth of my eye.

Stephen Cass (11)
Grove Park School

MY MAGIC BOX

My box is made of dragon scales of sparkling silver,
and seashells picked by white sharks' tails.

Its hinges are the arms of a butterfly.
It is lined with the shredded skin of a flying snake,
and a twinkling eye in a freezing snowdrop.

Inside my box, I keep a stripe of Saturn's ring
flying round the Earth's core, and
children's friendship, tied to a ribbon of gold.
I hide my box in a beaded thread of a golden heart.

Kayleigh Fitzpatrick (11)
Grove Park School

MY MAGIC BOX

My box is made of a slug's tooth and a
black music note, hanging off a mountain.
Its hinges are the light in the dark.
It is lined with the green flame of a fire
and the brains of the moon and sun.
Inside my box, I keep a cruise from planet to planet,
and bunches of love and hate.
I hide my box in the meaning of life.

David Stoneman-Merret (11)
Grove Park School

Dogs

Dogs can be wild,
like animals in the wild.
Dogs can be calm,
like people.
Dogs can be spotted
like leopards can be spotted.
Dogs can be plain
like a piece of plain paper.
Dogs can be big,
like people can be big.
Dogs can be small,
like wolves can be small.
Dogs can be fat,
like pigs can be fat.
Dogs can be thin,
like needles can be thin.
Dogs can be tall,
like giraffes can be tall.
Dogs can be short,
like people can be short.
Dogs can be noisy,
like nans can be noisy.
Dogs can be quiet,
like rabbits can be quiet.
Dogs can be messy,
like people can be messy.
Dogs can be clean,
like cats can be clean.
Dogs are cute.

Jessica Luckhurst (9)
Grove Park School

RABBITS

Rabbits here, rabbits there,
Furry rabbits everywhere.
Bobbing tails, pointed ears,
Bright button eyes gaze at the sky,
Quick as a flash they've all gone home for dinner,
Before it's all gone.

Brown bunnies,
White bunnies,
Black bunnies too,
Running up the hillside after me and you.

Jolene Hayre (9)
Grove Park School

MY MAGIC BOX

My box is made of the movement of the snowdrop
and the sketch of white in the money tree.
Its hinges are made of the centre of a flower
in a dog's bite.
It is lined with a smile of winter and the cold
of summer and the bird's jumper from Egypt.
Inside my box, I keep a turtle's shell on a dead ship
and the blood of the heart's berry.
I hide my box in a ball of lava which floats in space
and glows for all to see.

Kathryn Charlesworth (11)
Grove Park School

PENS

Pens, pens, pens galore,
I keep losing them, what a bore.
Pens, pens, pens galore.

When I go shopping,
The ink cartridges are popping
And the pens leak everywhere.

Pens, pens, pens galore,
I keep losing them, what a bore.
Pens, pens, pens galore.

Now I've got a brilliant pen,
When I'll lose it, who knows when?
So I got a spare one just in case.

Pens, pens, pens galore,
I keep losing them, what a bore.
Pens, pens, pens galore.

I thought the pen case was all sorted,
Now more pens are being imported.
Pens, pens, pens, what a bore.

Matthew Wedlake (9)
Grove Park School

SISTER

Zena is my sister,
She's very kind,
There is one thing she's always using,
And that's definitely her mind.

I love my sister dearly,
She's very, very sweet,
But what I really hate
Is the smell of her cheesy feet.

I have the bestest sister,
She's always by my side,
She can be kind of moody,
But always keeps her pride.

Her favourite colour's red,
She is not very big,
But very well fed.

Sonia Gardner (11)
Grove Park School

TIGERS

Tigers are scary,
Tigers are hairy,
Tigers are gigantic,
Tigers have sharp teeth,
Tigers have stripes,
Tigers are wild creatures,
Tigers have whiskers,
Tigers have fierce-looking eyes,
Tigers have long tails,
Tigers eat other animals,
Tigers are fast,
Tigers are fierce,
Tigers are orange,
Tigers have black stripes,
Tigers have pointed ears,
Tigers are mammals.

Daryl King (8)
Grove Park School

MY MAGIC BOX

My box is made of air and wishes,
Its hinges are a bird's nest,
It is lined with chocolate and milk.
Inside my box, I keep a summer's cool breeze.
I hide my box in a firework's spark.

Nadiya Hasan (11)
Grove Park School

CREEPILY

Creepily the trees sway back and forth,
Creepily the wind blows at night,
Creepily the beetle scuttles along the path,
Creepily the sea hits the stones,
Creepily the bee buzzes at dawn,
Creepily life goes on and on.

Kelly Langiano (9)
Herne CE Junior School

MY UNCLE STEPHEN

He loved me so,
How much he loved me I will never know,
As he died when I was a baby.
So many things there were to say.
In my family, all we have is tragic illness.
My great nan now sits in hospital,
Only a couple of years after my grandad.

Natisha Hart (10)
Herne CE Junior School

MY PAINTBOX

Gold is the colour of a one pound coin,
Or the colour of some gold earrings,
And the frame of someone's glasses.

Green is the colour of fresh, green grass,
Or the colour of a 7-Up can,
And the colour of the Jutes winning the cup.

White is the colour of clouds up in the sky,
Or the colour of a school shirt,
And the colour of a white board.

Red is the colour of danger,
Or is the colour of a red Porsche 911,
And red is the colour of Father Christmas.

Yellow is the colour of the glimmering sun,
Or the colour of Sunny Delight,
And yellow is the fourth colour in the rainbow.

Toby Andrews (9)
Herne CE Junior School

THE WRITER OF THIS POEM IS . . .

The writer of this poem is . . .
As dead as a zombie,
As heavy as a ton weight,
As flickery as a book,
More annoying than a sister!
As naughty as a hyena.
I am all these things, plus more!

Ben Moody (9)
Herne CE Junior School

My New Classroom

I opened the door to take a look,
I didn't know what to do.
There wasn't another child in the room,
So I felt even more new.
I sat down in my classroom smiling so sweet,
I really felt nervous so I looked at my feet.
The teacher showed me round,
but instead I looked at the ground.
'I want to go home' I said,
'No you can't,
you have to stay,
you can't go back home to bed.'
The classroom was okay,
I did enjoy it a bit.
I woke up, it was just a dream.
I can't wait to go to my new classroom
in the morning.

Janine Baybutt (9)
Herne CE Junior School

Sisters

Sisters, sisters, where do they come from?
Sisters, sisters, they are back again.
My sister thinks she's pretty but she isn't.
All sisters say they have a brain
But they have only got one cell.
Why do we have sisters?
But sometimes you get stuck with them.
                              (Silly sisters!)

Jessica Daniels
Herne CE Junior School

CAREFULLY

Carefully the dolphins dive
in and out of the waves.

Carefully, the sun puts
his hat on.

Carefully the flowers
sing in the sunlight.

Carefully I lay my head
on the safe pillow.

Carefully people pray to God.

Carefully we watch the birds
fly in the sunlight.

Carefully we care for one
another.

Abigail Blew (9)
Herne CE Junior School

THE WRITER OF THIS POEM IS . . .

The writer of this poem is . . .
As cool as ice,
As quick as a machine gun,
As funny as a clown,
Only sometimes
As good as silver, maybe,
As helpful as a pencil,
I think.

Ben Cox (8)
Herne CE Junior School

COLOURS OF THE WIND

Red is the colour of the sunset
Many a time in the evening light,
The colour of Po on a cold night.
Red is the colour of cherryade.

Purple is the colour of my suede shoes,
And many a time, my wallpaper.
The colour of Tinky Winky on a summer's day,
The colour of my life in years gone by.

White is the colour of the Furby I want for Christmas.
Snow fallen down the chimney.
Sniff the rat, running in his wheel.
White is the colour of flimsy paper.

Pink is the colour of Sniff's eyes on a dark night,
The colour of my nail varnish.

Cheryll Fenwick (10)
Herne CE Junior School

THE WRITER OF THIS POEM

The writer of this poem is . . .
As plain as a rubber,
As thin as a book,
As sharp as a knife,
As funny as a clown,
As noisy as an elephant,
As dead as a zombie.
The writer of this poem is me!

Emily Farquhar (9)
Herne CE Junior School

EIGHT ANGRY ANTS

Eight angry ants going for a walk
Splat went one and then there were seven.
Seven angry ants went to the park
One went to the toilet then there were six.
Six angry ants went to the zoo
One got eaten then there were five.
Five angry ants went to the town
One got ran over then there were four.
Four angry ants went to bed
One went under then there were three.
Three angry ants went out shopping
One got killed then there were two.
Two angry ants went fishing
One fell in and then there was one.
One angry ant fell off a horse
Then there was none.

William Parker (9)
Herne CE Junior School

QUIETLY

Quietly the mouse scuttles around,
Tries not to make a sound.
Quietly the wind blows past,
Quietly blowing the ship's mast,
Quietly we turn the page,
Quietly we open the rat's cage,
Quietly we do our work,
Trying our hardest not to smirk.

Nicola Keeble (10)
Herne CE Junior School

FIVE LITTLE BIRDS

Five little birds sitting in a tree,
One was poor,
Then there were four.
Four little birds sitting in a tree,
One got stuck,
Then there were three.
Three little birds sitting in a tree,
One went to the loo,
Then there were two.
Two little birds sitting in a tree,
One went to have a bun,
Then there was one.
One little bird sitting in a tree,
He bought a gun,
Then there were none.

Leo Johnston (9)
Herne CE Junior School

JACK-IN-THE-BOX

Sadly Jack sits in his box,
Unwanted by anybody.
Silently he cries himself to sleep,
But then he hears a noise!
He is lifted down from his shelf
And put in the back of a car.
He is moving.
Then at last, he is opened to the light,
A smiling face, a playful game.

Katie Sutton (10)
Herne CE Junior School

LIVERPOOL

Liverpool are the best football team in the world.
They run around the pitch like mad.
Michael Owen shoots a goal.
Never forget the players in the team.
They already have Paul Ince as the captain.
Oh what a wonderful team they are.
Never forget the colours, red and white.
They're the team you must never forget.
Grand, grand, grand Liverpool are.
They have won the FA Cup 1,000,000 times.
I support them wonderfully.
I write hundreds of stories and poems all the time.
Michael Owen's 18 years old.
He has never been banned from England.
Most of the other teams were not very good.

Nicholas Little (8)
Herne CE Junior School

MY TEACHER

My teacher is really nice.
He lets us throw rubbers around the room.
He flew over the school on a broom.
He lets us do backwards maths.
He even lets the boys play football in the classroom.
He wears funny clothes, he has a very big nose.
He wears big glasses, as big as a saucepan.
All my friends and I think he is really awesome.
I am really glad he is my teacher.

Alice Allwright (9)
Herne CE Junior School

On Easter Day

The writer of this poem is . . .
As sweet as a fluffy kitten,
As clever as a cat,
As happy as a small child,
As hungry as a goat,
As clumsy as the wind,
As fast as my thoughts,
As sharp as a lemon,
As young as a bud on a tree,
As cheeky as a hyena,
As hot as a dragon's flame and
As funny as a joke.
All of these things are hard to say, but,
This is what I'm like on Easter day!

Georgina Chapman (9)
Herne CE Junior School

Quietly

Quietly the mouse eats its cheese,
Quietly the sun sets in the breeze,
Quietly the plane flies in the sky,
Quietly the daffodils grow nearby,
Quietly the sea hits the cliff,
Quietly the clock goes tick, tick, tick,
Quietly the water comes out of the tap,
Quietly the flag goes flap, flap, flap.
Quietly, quietly.
Shhhhhhhh!

Gemma Davis (10)
Herne CE Junior School

THE WRITER OF THIS POEM IS . . .

The writer of this poem is . . .
As mischievous as a chimpanzee,
As great as a gold nugget,
As plain as a skirting board,
As good as a dormouse,
As frisky as a ferret.
The writer of this poem is . . .
As good as gems,
As cheeky as a monkey,
As noisy as an elephant,
As brave as a tiger,
And as strong as a cliff
But there's only one thing wrong,
I never do what I'm told to do!

Michael Page (8)
Herne CE Junior School

THE ROARING TIGER

The roaring tiger roars
and has very long claws.
The roaring tiger roars
in the middle of the night
it gives me a fright.
The roaring tiger roars
it sleeps in the day
and comes out at night.
The roaring tiger roars
and has very long claws.

Marie Newton (9)
Herne CE Junior School

WHEN I AM OLD I WILL . . .

When I am old, I will . . .
Wear a pink, sparkly cardigan and a
Luminous green knee-length skirt.
I will wear red shoes and dance
Until I fall asleep.
When I am old, I will die my hair each day,
So that it matches each outfit.
When I am old and I see young men,
I will pinch their bums.
When I am old, I will go to the bingo house
And kick all their boards off of the tables.
When I am old, I will go bowling and
Run down the allies.
When I am old.

Charlotte Hamilton (10)
Herne CE Junior School

HALLOWE'EN

When it was Hallowe'en I went to bed, I heard a noise
When I looked there was a ghost, the ghost was crying,
I said 'What's the matter?'
He said 'All the other ghosts don't like me.'
I said 'Why?'
'Because I am too small.'
So I went and caught them and I said
'Come here, can you stop picking on the little ghost?'
They said 'Okay.'
Then I went to bed.

Joss Wheeler (9)
Herne CE Junior School

THE WRITER OF THIS POEM

The writer of this poem is . . .
As jolly as a clown,
As cheeky as a rude joke,
As mischievous as a monkey,
As good as a trained dog,
As bold as a green t-shirt,
As noisy as an elephant,
As plain as a rubber.
It's all very well me writing all this.
Some ideas are very true,
Others aren't so true!
I propose to stay as noisy, jolly and cheeky,
So don't say 'Be good,' because I won't be!

Nicola Robertson (9)
Herne CE Junior School

THE WRITER OF THIS POEM IS . . .

The writer of this poem is . . .
As funny as a clown,
As quick as a flash,
As clever as a scientist,
As cheeky as a monkey,
As strong as a wall,
As mad as a hyena,
As cool as ice,
As helpful as my mum,
And all of this is true.

Drew Allen (8)
Herne CE Junior School

THE WRITER OF THIS POEM IS . . .

The writer of this poem is . . .
As funny as a doctor, doctor joke,
As strong as steel,
As fast as a cheetah,
As cheeky as a mouse.
The writer of this poem is . . .
As noisy as a monkey,
As tall as the Empire State Building,
As mischievous as a robber,
As good as a wise man,
As smelly as gas,
As dead as a doormat,
And as clever as can be!

Matthew Bubb (9)
Herne CE Junior School

THE WRITER OF THIS POEM IS . . .

The writer of this poem is . . .
As sharp as a knife,
As mean as a minx,
As lean as a lynx,
As funny as a clown,
As good as a puppy,
As right as a calculator,
As strong as a very big man.
I'm heavier than a door knob,
And as good as gold.
Oh, but I never ever do what I am told.

Ellen Jenkins (9)
Herne CE Junior School

MY MOUSE

My mouse is called Tom,
And my mouse is black,
My mouse is furry,
My mouse is cheerful,
My mouse is cute,
My mouse is cuddly,
My mouse is friendly,
My mouse is happy,
My mouse is soft,
My mouse is small,
And most of all,
My mouse is fun.

Thomas White (9)
Herne CE Junior School

THE GALLOPING HORSE

In the field I see a very nice site indeed
A white horse as white as snow
Wearing a pink bow.
As it gallops round and round
I hear its hooves
Clatter, clackety-clack, clackety-clack.
Eating grass as green as can be.
It smiles at me so sweetly.
The evening sun sets, it's time to go.
But wait, what's this I see?
A horse waiting just for me.

Chloe Louise Nicholson (9)
Herne CE Junior School

COLOURS

Purple is the colour of frustration,
Or juicy grapes,
And plumbs, ripe and yum.

Gold is a good party, loads of fun,
Or a short, flashy dress,
And fun that you have every day.

Silver is the stars, bright in the night,
Or glitter, sparkly everywhere,
And the colour of peaceful evenings.

Dark blue is the colour of an evening sky,
Or the calmness of an evening in summer,
And the romance of two people kissing at night.

White is the colour of blank, not knowing,
Or winter with nothing at all,
And a freshly made bed with white sheets.

Black is death, sad and long,
Or cross people with a mind full of cross thoughts,
And a pirate's disgusting black teeth.

Beige is the colour of every grain of sand,
Or summer's hot sun,
And beige is a happy colour.

Alanna Henderson (10)
Herne CE Junior School

MY FIENDISH LITTLE SISTER

My fiendish
little sister
went
for
a
wee
I
locked
her in
so
she
could
stop
teasing
me
But
perhaps
I should
let
her
out
I
don't
care
if
she
teases
me.

Adam Christopher Parker (9)
Herne CE Junior School

ROBOTS EVERYWHERE

Robots here
Robots there
Robots are everywhere
In the computer
On your telly
In your bedroom eating jelly
I'd like to have a robot
Robots here
Robots there
Robots are everywhere.

Jamie Parker (8)
Herne CE Junior School

PARENTS

Parents
they're moody.
Pain, aggravating, bossy.
Like kings and queens that order
their servants to do things for them.
Like pigs at a trough.
I feel disgusted.
It's like watching animals killing
their prey.
Parents
They're just aggravating bosses.

Melanie Hatcher (11)
Hoo St Werburgh CP School, Rochester

A Teacher

A teacher
She teaches people
She's funny, helpful, nice to us
She's like a hen watching her chicks
She's like a mum watching first born babies
She's kind and patient
Like a virtuous saint.
A teacher
Makes me feel good.

Martin James (11)
Hoo St Werburgh CP School, Rochester

Pens

Come in all colours
bright, colourful ink.
Writes like river flows
like a feather on a swan.
Useful in all ways
like fish that needs water.
Pens,
the writers of truth.

Andrew Chilcott (11)
Hoo St Werburgh CP School, Rochester

WAR EVACUEES!

Sitting at the station
Waiting for the train
Everybody's crying
Then it starts to rain

The sirens call their warning
We all run inside
I hope no one dies

We say our last goodbyes
Then mother starts to cry
I tell her not to worry
And I'll be back in a hurry

The train starts moving
I take a last look and mother is
Clutching my favourite book.

Natalie Bishop (11)
Hoo St Werburgh CP School, Rochester

THE OCEAN

The ocean,
blue as can be,
dark, gloomy and cold,
as cold as ice
and as dark as night.
I feel that I could freeze in it,
like an ice cube in a glass of Coke.
The ocean,
freezing, deep, mysterious.

Ashley Lennox (10)
Hoo St Werburgh CP School, Rochester

EVACUEE!

I was sent from the city
to the countryside.
Before I left I cried and cried
But now I've been gone for
about a week.
I'm getting braver I'm starting
to speak.
My new guardians are okay
But I wish I could go back home today.
I wish the war would finish right now.
I wonder who started it?
I wonder how.
I often think how grown ups can fight.
They're supposed to co-operate and be civilised
But now I'm thinking how and why
People want to make others die.

Julia Diss (10)
Hoo St Werburgh CP School, Rochester

KIND FRIENDS!

Kind friends
Who never let you drown,
Nice, loving and generous
They're like guards who never let you get hurt,
They're like something that's caught its prey
And won't let you go.
I feel really happy
I'm like a jolly clown who's never sad.
Kind friends
Reminds us how important friends are.

Rachael Forde (11)
Hoo St Werburgh CP School, Rochester

BATTLE

Some battles are just not worth it
they only cause hurt, like
you stole my pencil,
I want to go out,
He's *my* best friend,
You called me a strawberry tree!
I don't want you to copy my work,
> *or*

Important battles, that if you give in,
could make you very sorry, like
I don't want to smoke - you can't make me,
Should I have another drink? I will be driving.
It could end up to be very dangerous.

But whatever battles you come up against
In life it's *your* choice what *you* do.

Paul Williams (11)
Hoo St Werburgh CP School, Rochester

OCEANS

Ocean,
Salty,
Big, spacious, dangerous.
As cold as an iceberg,
its bottom as dark as a cave.
Small and inferior,
tiny like an ant.
Ocean
Deadly tides, beware!

Leah Lewis (10)
Hoo St Werburgh CP School, Rochester

TODAY IS THE DAY

The letter came today that my
father is going away.
I wonder whether he'll survive
Oh I do hope that I will stay alive.
Then the next day I found out
that I had to go away.
I got sent to the country
where I might have to stay.
Then one fearful horrid night
a bomb dropped on
the house down the street,
among the rubble I saw a head
and a gruesome pair of feet.
I now know that war
should be against the *law!*

Sarah Ashdown (11)
Hoo St Werburgh CP School, Rochester

WORLD WAR II

World War II
Ended fifty-four years ago
Horrific, gloomy, terrifying
Like pit bulls fighting
Like losing a loved relative
British men and women were very brave
Like a fireman in an inferno
World War II
Reminds me of fighting for peace.

Billy Humphrey (11)
Hoo St Werburgh CP School, Rochester

GOING AWAY

I was sitting at the window
Watching my dad and the soldiers
going off to war.

Then I am at the station with a
gas mask on my shoulder
and a label round my neck.

Saying goodbye to my mother
and giving her my last kiss
tears are running down my face
as the train is pulling away.

I think about my mother every day
and wonder if I would ever
see her again!

Laura Blake (11)
Hoo St Werburgh CP School, Rochester

WHY?

Bombs exploding
sirens roaring
guns firing
Why?
all this killing
all this dying
all this hatred
Why . . .?
Because it's war.

Adam Carter (10)
Hoo St Werburgh CP School, Rochester

WAR

Sitting in the kitchen
Sitting on the floor
Watching all the soldiers
Going off to war.

Sitting on the train
Waving goodbye
Crying again
I hope I won't die.

I see all the people
Lying on the ground
Crying out in pain
Then not making a sound.

Charlotte Broadhurst (11)
Hoo St Werburgh CP School, Rochester

WHAT IS HAPPENING?

Watching from the window
Feeling all alone
Seeing people dying and just feel like crying.

Adults arguing night and day and tell
Their children they have to go away.

I now know that Hitler is coming because
I can hear the doodlebugs humming.

I have a fear of losing someone near
and war to me is still not clear.

Ashley Chambers (11)
Hoo St Werburgh CP School, Rochester

WAR

War is even worse than it seems.
Why do we have war?
Because war is;

People screaming,
people crying,
people shouting,
Bang!
Death,
fighting,
destruction,
pain,
suffering,
innocent people getting killed,
houses getting wiped out,
England Vs Germany,
torture,
loud noises everywhere,
bombs going off,
and
defeat.

Gemma Yard (10)
Hoo St Werburgh CP School, Rochester

THE MIGHTY BEAR

The mighty bear, dark, brown, hairy, grizzly,
with sharp claws.
Its coat is like a velvet curtain
and features like my angry teacher.
I would feel nervous like a tree going to be cut in half.
Mighty bears feature teeth like razors, beware!

James Barnett (11)
Hoo St Werburgh CP School, Rochester

PEAS

Peas
They're round
They're green, little
and jump around in
our mouths.
They're like
leather footballs
or muddy meatballs,
fresh as daisies.
Peas,
like all your
friends in a pod.

Tom Bucklen (11)
Hoo St Werburgh CP School, Rochester

WAR IS FOOTBALL

War is like a
game of football
someone dies a
goal is scored
when they're shot
it was a foul
do you know why
war started?

Who knows!

Ben Mansell (11)
Hoo St Werburgh CP School, Rochester

GOODBYE

Waiting at the harbour
My parents by my side.
My bag over my shoulder
My gas mask in my hand.
The boat pulled into the harbour,
I'm climbing on the ramp.
I'm stepping on the ramp
I'm stepping on the deck
I'm waiting at the side.
The boat pulled out from the harbour
I wave goodbye as my parents
get smaller and smaller.

Clare Fray (10)
Hoo St Werburgh CP School, Rochester

THE ADDER

Adder,
it slithers
small, poisonous, killer,
hissing like a garden hose,
long as string,
worried, frightened,
scared as a child's first day
at school.
Adder,
slimy, horrid snake.

Christine Vant (11)
Hoo St Werburgh CP School, Rochester

WAR

War
people dying
guns, aeroplanes, bombs.
People dying for their country
Mums and dads arguing,
it makes me feel sad,
I hurt.
Sad as a child who
has lost its family.
War,
it reminds us how
precious our lives are.

Shane Lewis (10)
Hoo St Werburgh CP School, Rochester

BOYS

Not all boys are horrible,
99.5 per cent are,
ugly,
mad,
loud,
rude,
big headed,
and
0.5 per cent are OK.
Boys!

Natalie Watkins (11)
Hoo St Werburgh CP School, Rochester

FRIENDS

Friends,
They're like brothers
Kind, helpful and friendly.
They make me feel like
I have got a heart of gold.
They stick together like
lions eating their prey.
They're the best thing in school.
We are like peas in a pod.
Friends,
They never let you down.

Thomas Deadman (11)
Hoo St Werburgh CP School, Rochester

WAR

Bang
Whoosh
bombs sounding like a lion's roar
guns going off
sirens sounding like people screaming
thunder lightning
Germans ahead
planes flying 100,000 miles per hour
dying shooting
people lost
it's war.

Anthony Green (10)
Hoo St Werburgh CP School, Rochester

FIRE

It burns
orange, red and yellow
like the devil in hell.
As warm as toast
I am frightened and scared
As scared as a big fire
Burning in furnaces, melting metal.

Adam Dewar (11)
Hoo St Werburgh CP School, Rochester

THE SEA

The sea,
cold, gloomy, blue and dark.
Colder than an ice cube.
Unfriendly like a giant.
I feel lost like a wandering lamb.
The sea,
desolate, daunting place.

Jamie Jewell (11)
Hoo St Werburgh CP School, Rochester

WAR!

The sound of bombs echoing continuously in my mind
People yelling like big baboons
Children crying like a dog without a master
Flags flying like fish tails wiggling
Sirens screeching like nails scratching on a blackboard
But war is just like war.

Owen Anderson (10)
Hoo St Werburgh CP School, Rochester

TITANIC

Titanic
Sunk 1912.
Huge, sad, mighty.
As enormous as a mountain.
As large as a giant.
It makes me sad, depressed,
like low tide.
Titanic
reminds us that lives
are wasted.

Fern Dutton (11)
Hoo St Werburgh CP School, Rochester

FOOTBALLERS

Footballers,
run around the field all day,
kicking, sliding, playing.
As tall as skyscrapers,
as wide as a bus.
They make me feel unskilful,
as unskilful as a man tied up.
Footballers,
they make me think of perfect idols.

Kirsty Reach (11)
Hoo St Werburgh CP School, Rochester

THE KNIFE

The knife
It slices things up,
Sharp, shiny and long.
Shiny as gold
Flashes like lightning
It gives me the creeps.
I feel as scared as a mouse
What a killer, it makes me feel sick.

Lauren Clarke (10)
Hoo St Werburgh CP School, Rochester

WAR!

You know war is bad, women feeling sad,
Husbands risking their lives, how could they leave their wives?
Hitler trying to rule the world, not making any peace at all.
The sound of war is a terrible thing, the evacuation bells ring,
The sad, sad songs people sing, children getting sent away,
Through the war, they have to stay! Children die, parents die
It's a bloody sight!

Alex Dyzart (10)
Hoo St Werburgh CP School, Rochester

WAR!

War is full of people dying
War has many people crying
War is sad
War is bad
So why do we fight and disagree?
We should live together in harmony.

Lianne Watts (10)
Hoo St Werburgh CP School, Rochester

WAR

Saying bye to mother
giving her my last kiss
I wonder when I'll see her again
surely I'll be missed.

Tears run down my face
as the train pulls away
children waving to families
they won't see the next day.

I think about my mother
and the people left behind
then about where I am and
what I'm going to find.

I get more scared as I enter the house
the one I'm staying in
I am in the country and the lady and man take me to my room.
I run straight in and just cry and cry.
Why does there have to be a war?

Emma Griffiths (10)
Hoo St Werburgh CP School, Rochester

WAR

War
Innocent people dying
Bloodthirsty, deafening, fighting
Like wrestlers in a ring they fight
Wounded people crying like babies
No one needs war
I feel as sick as a dog at the thought of war
No one needs to die.

Craig Watts (10)
Hoo St Werburgh CP School, Rochester

GRASS

Grass
Grass is green
Soft, long and luscious
And as fresh as a daisy
And as large as space.
I feel that the grass is delightful
I feel like a pig in mud.
Grass
Never-ending supply.

Gemma Knight (11)
Hoo St Werburgh CP School, Rochester

THE FREEZE BREEZE

I can numb your hands,
I can make you freeze,
I can make you cold,
I can swirl the leaves of the trees.

I can freeze your hand,
I can whip your face,
I can whiff your hair,
All over the place.

I can sting your eyes,
I can blow your body,
I can redden your ears,
I can make you sorry!

Hannah Sharpless (11) & Amy Griggs (10)
Joy Lane Junior School

?

Is a butterfly something
  You spread on toast
      Followed by jam?
        Does a
         spider
          spy on
          you, when
         you turn
         around?
     Is a dragonfly a dragon
     that's just small,
     or just a fly that breathes
     fire?
     Is a dogfish
     a dog, that
     just swims
     around?

     Does a
     swordfish
     really fight duels
     for damsels in
     distress?

Amy Lucy (11)
Joy Lane Junior School

SCHOOL

School is the best place
You learn things there fast
Like this work I've written.

Joseph Masters (8)
Joy Lane Junior School

THE KNIGHT

Knight, knight
King of the knights
When soldiers have a sight of you
You give them a fright
Without any fight.

Shield at the ready
Standing steady,
That king of the night
That gave the soldiers a fright
With his sword raised as high as a kite,
Shining in the moonlight.

His big sturdy horse
Set on course
To ride in force
With his army of dwarfs.

A king of old
With a heart of gold
Although he is very bold
Who wouldn't sell his kingdom
For any amount of gold.

Daniel Lamba (9)
Joy Lane Junior School

SEA

Wave crasher
Flood maker
Glass smoother
Fish home
Inflatable taker.

Lucy Gustafson (11)
Joy Lane Junior School

CRAB POEM

When I scuttle by the sea
people are always scared of me.
I only pinch, I'm not vicious
so why are people always suspicious.
Please let me live by the sea
and I beg you not to eat me.
I've got a shell that protects me
so will you please just leave me be.
I've only got little clippers
so you can tread on them
with your huge slippers.

Ben Croucher (10)
Joy Lane Junior School

THE MAGIC FAIRY

A beautiful fairy, there it was,
Asleep on a lily,
Peaceful it was,
Calm water flowing down a lake,
The lily pad was awake,
The fairy had awoke,
Her beautiful wings had shook
She was lovely and white,
She had a fright.

Freyja Ambler (10)
Joy Lane Junior School

THE SPACESHIP

A spaceship with L-plates came juddering down
And flattened a cornfield a few miles from town,
Out stepped an alien, Zozimus Glop,
Who had grievously botched his emergency stop,
An earthling could fly this crate better than you;
His examiner bellowed, her head turning blue,
As she shouted she noticed (congealing with fear)
A quivering figure, 'Hoy! Come over here.'
And the figure (a schoolgirl Madeline Pike)
Came tottering over still pushing its bike,
Inside the examiner barked 'Come this way,
I'll train you to fly by the end of the day!'

Billy McNamara (9)
Joy Lane Junior School

ANGER

Screaming children
Scary frown,
Monstrous roar,
Burning face,
Clenched fist,
Spitting fire,
Grinding teeth,
Wild eyes.

Simon Fosbraey (11)
Joy Lane Junior School

BORING LESSONS

How I hate science lessons,
Geography is even worse.
Art, I find is quite that boring,
Poetry I can't write a verse.

Maths I can't work out anything,
History is much too mad.
I can't wait till hometime,
School is really bad.

Now I am at home,
It is really good.
I don't want to go to school,
Even though I should.

Christopher Edwards (7)
Joy Lane Junior School

HELL

A grave's grime
A death wish
A ghost's wrath
The demon's face
A tomb carver
A fire's rage
The gloomy caves
The dripping blood
The wooden coffins
A gory death
A devil's fork.

Adam Davidge (11)
Joy Lane Junior School

THE KNIGHT

There was a knight called Dave,
Who was very very brave.
He was tall and strong,
And as he rode along,
He saw a gloomy cave.

He heard a damsel in distress,
He thought she might have met a pest.
He galloped round
To where he heard the sound,
And found the damsel in a mess.

'I went into the cave,' she cried,
'I heard a noise and tried to hide.'
'I'll save you,' said brave Dave.
So he jumped off his horse and charged inside.

You could hear a mighty fight,
Then out ran the fearless knight.
He screamed and shouted,
His horse he mounted,
And galloped off in fright.

Then a mouse came out,
And the damsel gave a shout
But Dave just rode away,
Too scared to save the day,
Of that there is no doubt.

Sarah Gilbert (8)
Joy Lane Junior School

THE KNIGHT

Here I am the bright, white knight.
My plunging horse with flaring nostril,
Eager to be off.

I side-step round the lesser men
And bow to king and queen,
Then off across the chequered fields
To face the ebony foe.

I quickly dodge the holy man
With crook and mitred hat

But then a big black bird, a rook,
Looks set to capture me.
To him as well I give the slip
And then I see my chance:

A fearsome glance,
A neigh, a prance,
I push aside the queen.
Then face to face
At last I come
And hold the king in check.

'Get out of that!'
'I fear I can't!'
'I thought you couldn't,'
'Mate!'

James Blakebrough (9)
Joy Lane Junior School

EARTH

Earth.
What has become
Of this place;
It's developed into a
Disgrace.
We humans are
responsible;
We've made everything
Disposable.
Instead of recycling
Our junk,
We just let our rubbish
Pile and gunk,
The plants the fields
and trees;
The farms the seas
the bumblebees.
We've turned
Everything into a
Disgrace;
All caused by the
human race.
Earth,
What has become
Of this place?

David Humphreys (11)
Joy Lane Junior School

LOVE IS ...

A red heart,
Some deep romance,
A string of dates,
A strange stare,
Fluttering eyelashes,
A smiling face.

Nicola Cox (11)
Joy Lane Junior School

THE DANGERS

Inside a volcano,
Hot lava bubbles.
Anxious people,
From nearby villages,
Hear the warning.

They gather their possessions,
And flee.
Cars are stuck,
In traffic jams,
Horns hooting.

All of a sudden,
A loud rumble.
It shatters the air.
Everybody in the path of the lava,
Screams.

Gabriella Coombe (11)
Junior King's School

THE EARTH AND ME

Crashing waves as tall as a skyscraper,
Currents which flow like tons of confetti,
A deepening whirlpool as great as a manor,
And there's me, a small ripple in the blue.

A hurling fire that streaks across the land,
A tornado which torments trees of all kinds,
An earthquake which all buildings fall to,
And there's me, a gentle breeze in an autumn wood.

Massive storms which havoc the skies,
Huge hurricanes which birds fall prey to,
The odd meteorite which comes searing
                            through the sky,
And there's me, a cloud which moves across
                                    the Earth.

Alex Sanné (11)
Junior King's School

MY CAT

She sleeps all day,
Lazy and tired.
Suddenly it's midnight,
The full moon's out.
Off she goes through the fields
We call and call for her,
Finally morning comes
A surprise is waiting on the front porch.

A mouse!

Olivia Byrne (11)
Junior King's School

ANIMALS IN ME

There is a bear in me . . .
Raging in the wilderness . . .
Destructive beast tearing everything in its path
The savage animal impatient dangerous
But I can't let it go!

There is a shark in me . . .
Swiftly passing through the water . . .
The powerful jaws ready to kill, deadly
But I have to control it!

There is a hawk in me . . .
Eagerly watching its prey . . .
Gracefully swooping down on it
It is a deadly and quick killer!

Joshua Maley (11)
Junior King's School

INSIDE MY HEAD

Inside my head . . .
there is no brain,
just cricket, cricket, cricket.
My brain is protected
by that of pads and gloves,
thoughts in my head
are of Barbados,
where cricket is life.
My head dreams
of playing there,
in that far off
distant land . . .

William Bruce (11)
Junior King's School

INSIDE MY HEAD

Inside my head is a box of secrets,
fighting to get out.

There is a wild mustang prancing
in a tropical rainforest with a purple orange,
and a green cockatoo for an audience.

Swimming in my pool of thoughts
is a leopard coated dolphin chasing a gorilla
along the sea bed.

Amongst the happiness there is a graveyard
haunting me at night
But,
to help me I have my sunny island
where I sleep and relax.

Anna Broxup (11)
Junior King's School

A TRAIN

A rail follower
A sea underpasser
A weather reflector
A comfortable carrier
A mail transporter
A station stopper
A fast runner
A thinking controller
A car copier
A mean traveller . . .
                    A train.

Poppy Mitchell (11)
Junior King's School

MISS PERFECT

Her hair is neatly brushed back
Every individual strand in its place,
No trace of dirt can be magnified
And her eyelashes are separated with that sickening mascara.
Her nails are painted light blue and every delicate brush stroke
Can be seen on her perfectly filed nails.
She must excuse herself in every lesson to brush her long,
Strawberry blond hair and straighten her uniform -
But the teachers don't complain
Because she's perfect.
She must polish her high-heeled shoes twice a day
And change her gold earrings.
She wears a mini skirt to discos
To show off her long, slim, perfect legs.
When the boys fight over her
She beams a perfect smile.

Joanna Brilliant (11)
Junior King's School

ADULTS

Nagging nannies to nag at your bed,
Accurate aunties to educate you,
Fat fathers to make you eat,
Mad mothers to moan at your fat.

Good godfathers to wish you health,
Nodding nobles to guard your house,
Big brothers to beat you up,
Scared sisters to run and cry.

Cooking chefs to cook your food,
Standing servants to serve your food,
Top trainers to improve on your speed,
Vile villains to rip your veins.

Killing knights to kill enemies,
Old opticians to look at your eyes,
Cool cleaners to clean your sinks,
M . . . menacing me to muck around.

Timothy Leung (10)
Junior King's School

LION

It's a lazy sleeper
It's a crazy creeper
But a cute thing

It's a mad attacker
It's a glad defender
But a cool guy

It's a hairy animal
It's a sly nightmare
But a strong destroyer

It's a clever runner
It's a cruel catcher
But a Roaring King of the Jungle.

Roar.

Joshua Blinston Jones (10)
Junior King's School

A Trip To The Bottom Of The Sea

Standing in Whitstable harbour,
Rain splintering down on my face.
A solitary boat bouncing
Up and down on the rough, dull sea,
With clouds as black as soot.
Foaming waves crashing against the rocks.
The boat was drawn towards the rocks,
Like a magnet.
Then, without warning, it was lifted,
Hurled,
Then *crash,*
The boat smashed into a hundred pieces
And sunk beneath the raging sea,
To rest peacefully on the seabed.

James Lynes (10)
Junior King's School

140 Mph In A Car

He was driving at 140 mph in a car.
Over a country road
nobody could stop him.
It was like he was on the run.

He was going round a corner
when suddenly a Ford appeared.
The lady in the Ford
suddenly started to swing and sway.

She was too late.
The car had hit the railings and it was
smashed!
And I was not surprised it happened.

Elsa Butrous (10)
Junior King's School

A Boy's Mind

There is,
A mad robot,
Eating my maths homework,
And an idea,
For snake and kidney pie.

There is,
A blue cow,
Floating in the lava,
Of a swamp.

There is,
A multi-purpose moon,
A plug-in battery,
A square circle.

There is an alien,
Stealing a thief,
And a Hindu jumper,
Worn by the television.

It just cannot shrink,
Even when boiled or fried.

This is part of the mind,
A thousandth of the imagination,
Inside a boy's head,
Inside my head.

Philip Spicer (10)
Junior King's School

HOMELESS

I'm always on the streets,
Begging in the subways,
Sleeping in the parks,
I've been homeless all my life.

I'm never in a house,
I've never been to school,
I've never had a friend,
I've been homeless all my life.

I can't remember my parents,
They might have just walked past,
But they might be in a grave,
I've been homeless all my life.

If only I had £10,
I could get a decent meal,
Or some clothes that are warm,
I've been homeless all my life.

If only somebody took pity on me,
I could be much better off,
At least with better shelter,
I've been homeless all my life.

But I'm only a simple being on the streets,
And nobody will take me in.

I've been homeless all my life!

Can *you* help?

Craig Anthony Sawyer (10)
Junior King's School

HE WAS . . .

He was . . .
Short tempered
A manipulator
An optimist

He was . . .
A violin player
A music lover
A good singer

He was . . .
Generous
A giver not a taker
A money spender

He was . . .
A potato lover
A charming man
Popular with women

He was
A small man
A strong man
A good person
A family lover

He was . . .
Unfair at times
A strong decision maker
A picker of his favourites

He was . . .
My beloved grandfather.

Olenka Hamilton (11)
Junior King's School

THE PATRONISER

The way he pretends to know you so well.
The way he treats you like you
Can't make your own decisions.
The way you can't fight back
Because he's an adult and you're a child.

His walk! Nose in the air, sickly smile.
His exaggerated friendliness.
The 'No I'm sure Harry wouldn't want to do that.
It looks far too dangerous,' smiling
The whole time.

And everyone knows,
They're just too polite to tell him to stop.
And you're helpless.

He pushes you into things with his way
Of making you feel embarrassed
And then you're embarrassed anyway.

He knows you know.
He revels in it.
You can hear his silent laughter.

Harry Lancaster (11)
Junior King's School

FOOTBALLS

Lots of little footballs
Standing in a row
One fell over
Oh no!

Callum Costa (7)
Northdown CP School

PARENTS NEVER LISTEN

I love my bubblegum,
watch me blow a bubble.
If I blew one at you,
I would only get in trouble.

I hate having a bath,
do you like to?
Wet splashing water,
get it on the floor.

I hate doing homework,
rip it all up now.
Do not do any of it,
don't show it to our mums.

Roxanne Trent (8)
Northdown CP School

SNOW

In the morning
When I wake up
I look out the window
It is totally white
I get my clothes on
I went downstairs
Got my breakfast
Step outside
Make a snowman
Get hat and scarf
Even a carrot
I say to myself
It looks very good.

James Steven Brown (8)
Northdown CP School

FOOTBALL 2000

When I play football I always always score
No matter in wind, rain or sun
My life is so, so fun.

I speed up the field
I dribble the ball, I cross
I pass and then I score
And much much more.

When I play football I always always score
No matter in wind, rain or sun
My life is so, so fun.

When I go to bed
I dream of the World Cup final
In penalty knockout Ted's missed
It's up to me and I hit the post.

When I play football I always always score
No matter wind, rain or sun
My life is so, so fun.

I hit the post, I've got a rebound
I hit the crossbar
I wish I had a big, big Mars bar,
And then I missed
I'm lucky it was only a dream
But what if it wasn't.

When I play football I always always score
No matter in wind, rain or sun
My life is so, so fun.

Ten years later
In the World Cup
I hit the post
And then I score.

Ty Fairbrother (9)
Northdown CP School

RED MONSTER

The red monster
Lives under my bed
He crept out
And he made me scared
The sun melted the monster
All that was left was
Red claws.

Paul Hodges (7)
Northdown CP School

RED BALLOON

From a party
I got a red balloon
It was big
It floats up in the air
My face turns red as I run with my balloon
It pops
My face goes red when I cry.

David Wraight (7)
Northdown CP School

ONE SUNNY MORNING

One sunny morning the birds were eating leaves,
The tree had toilet paper hanging down on it.
A dog was saying miaow, miaow, and the cat was barking.

The clouds were snowing, the grass was shrinking,
The sun was raining, the people were crying.
What is happening to all these things?
A bear came along and shouted 'Be quiet, be quiet.'

They all went quiet,
'Why are you doing silly things?'
'We don't know,
We don't know!'
But then,
The sky went dark,
The moon came out.
Dark clouds came out,
The creatures said 'We just don't know.'
The creatures all went to sleep,
The bear went home,
It isn't really night-time, or is it?
Ssssh.

Marianne Hollins (9)
Northdown CP School

MISS MARSH

Somebody is knocking at the door.
Who is it? I hope it is not Miss Marsh.
She's old and scary, she's got a girl
called bobby who is hairy.
Miss Marsh's Bobby hasn't got any hobbies.

Becky Elks (8)
Northdown CP School

CATS ARE FLUFFY

A misty morning and the sun was following a cat
I like cats but I don't know why.

Cats are sweet
Cats are cute, cats, cats, cats.

Cats are bright. Cats are my favourite
and sometimes different colours.

Cats are sweet
Cats are cute, cats, cats, cats.

Cats come from lots of countries
and are sometimes funny.

Cats are sweet,
Cats are cute, cats, cats, cats.

Cats are funny, cats are naughty.
Cats, cats, cats.

Cats are sweet,
Cats are cute, cats, cats, cats.

Cats are fluffy, cats are cute,
Cats are noisy but sweet.

Cats are sweet,
Cats are cute, cats, cats, cats.

Katie Burke (8)
Northdown CP School

ONE FROSTY MORNING

One frosty morning
I saw a dog
By a frog
A boy called Bart
Who eats bark
Bart protects dogs.
He saw the dog
So he got a log for the dog.
Bart was whining for food.
The dog thought you have to whinge for food
So he did.
The dog caught a frog
By a log when the snow melted.

Alan Bennett (8)
Northdown CP School

YELLOW

Yellow is the sun that's in the sky.
Yellow are the books that I like to buy,
Yellow is for Nana when she eats her dinner,
Yellow is for leader when we are winners,
Yellow is the tin which I use as a cup,
Yellow is for box which is the shape of a square,
Yellow is for pencil which I like to share,
Yellow is for clock that likes to tick-tock,
Yellow is for light when it is night.

Amanda Wellard (8)
Northdown CP School

BEAUTIFUL THINGS THAT I HAVE SEEN

Beautiful things that I have seen
like wonders from a dream.
Daffodils, roses and tulips
all from the field so green.
Sometimes I think of you and wish
that you could be here.
To my surprise you are here and
getting smaller and smaller.

Think of castles and wonder what
I would be.
Before me in gold and silver
becomes a castle for me.

There in armour before the door
will be soldiers to keep people
away from me.
I wake up, my dream has faded away.

Lianne Ramshaw (9)
Northdown CP School

RED

Red apples grow on trees
Red tomato sauce on my peas
Blood is in my body
I can't find any in Noddy
I have red sweets for my treat
Red apples I eat for my sweet
Red is the chair which I sit on
Red is the book that I have torn.

Cara Downer (8)
Northdown CP School

ALIENS

Aliens, scary aliens, funny with funny guns.
Alien eyes, alien body. Aliens from Mars, aliens from Saturn.

Mars, Saturn, aliens are coming!
Run, run, run, run for your lives.

Leave Earth and go to the Arctic and the North Pole.
Aliens living in spaceships from Mars and Saturn.

Mars, Saturn, aliens are coming.
Run, run, run, run for your life.

In space plants and meteorites passing by.
Aliens small, aliens big, spaceships long, spaceships small.

Mars, Saturn, aliens are coming!
Run, run, run, run for your lives.

Ashley Knight (8)
Northdown CP School

MONSTERS

M onsters have green teeth
O n Monday monsters turn yellow
N oon monster come out to play
S oon a monster will eat me
T take a bite off my head
E at me up now
R obots eat monsters
S oon the monster was all gone.

Maria Adkins (9)
Northdown CP School

RED BALLOON

A red balloon is floating in the sky
The red balloon burst
Red rain sprinkling down
It fell into the road
A red car zoomed by
And squashed it flat.

Edward Ayres (8)
Northdown CP School

YELLOW

Yellow is the sun bright like a star.
Yellow is the banana I ate in my car.
Yellow is the sunflower looking at me.
Yellow is the honey made by the bee.
Yellow is the sand beneath my toes.
Yellow is the paint, I blob on my nose.

Jemma Hills (8)
Northdown CP School

GREEN

Green is the grass I like to play.
Green is the peas that I eat all day.
Green is the seaweed all wet and smelly.
Green is the leaves I jump on with my welly.
Green is the caterpillar that crawls around.
Green is the tree I plant in the ground.

Kayleigh Hammond (8)
Northdown CP School

GREEN

Green are the grapes that I eat,
Green are the leaves under my feet,
Green are the apples that hang on the trees,
Green is the seaweed around my knees,
Green is the mouldy cheese that I see,
Green are the peas for you and me.

Jodi Bovington (7)
Northdown CP School

YELLOW

Yellow is the honey that's made by bees,
Yellow is the budgie that sits on my knee,
Yellow is like a flower that grows in the ground,
Yellow is a scarf that I wrap all around,
Yellow is the paint that I like to see,
Yellow is the honey that's made by bees.

Samantha Buttigieg (7)
Northdown CP School

YELLOW

Yellow is the sun shining on me,
Yellow are the chips I have for tea,
Yellow is the yolk of the egg I eat,
Yellow is the paint on the garden seat,
Yellow are the chicks newly born,
Yellow is the coat that is badly torn.

Kyle Easton (8)
Northdown CP School

PURPLE

Purple are the grapes that I like to eat,
Purple is the cushion on my comfy seat,
Purple is my coat I put on when it's cold,
Purple is my boat that is not very old,
Purple is Tinky Winky who I watch on my TV,
Purple is the bruise I get on my knee,
When I fall when I'm climbing a big, big tree.

Lee Fairbrother (7)
Northdown CP School

RAIN

R ain is cold
A nd it gets us wet
I t tastes like water
N ever ever nice blue sky.

Kayleigh Ward (8)
Northdown CP School

FOOTBALL FANTASY

F ootball is a game,
O nly it's for fame.
O wen gets goals for England,
T o help them win the cup.
B ournemouth are going up
A nd win the league.
L eeds are doing well.
L eeds are sponsored by Packard Bell.

Lee Ludlow (8)
Parkwood Junior School

TEN MOULDY ALIENS

Ten mouldy aliens
Going out to dine,
One fell off the chair
And then there were nine.

Nine mouldy aliens
Walking out of the gate,
One drowned in the milk bottle,
And then there were eight.

Eight mouldy aliens
Walking down to Devon,
One walked off the track,
And then there were seven.

Seven mouldy aliens
Eating a Double Twix,
One floated right away
And then there were six.

Six mouldy aliens
Learning how to dive,
One lost his swimming trunks
And then there were five.

Five mouldy aliens
Sitting on the floor,
One got carpet burns
And then there were four.

Four mouldy aliens
Going for some tea,
One got scalded badly
And then there were three.

Three mouldy aliens
Going to the loo,
One got flushed away,
And then there were two.

Two mouldy aliens
Sucking their thumbs,
One sucked too hard
And then there was one.

One mouldy alien
Going to the sun,
He got burnt to ashes
And then there were none.

Amy Millbank (10)
Parkwood Junior School

HORSES!

Horses in the summer sun
Standing in a line,
Shadows sparkling like the stars
For horses having fun.

Horses in the wind, wet air,
Scavenging through the woods,
Stars like flying horses
At a party flowing indoors.

Galloping little horses in the frozen snow,
Getting frozen to their toes -
Hooves glittering in the snow,
All the horses galloping slow.

Natalie Filmer (11)
Parkwood Junior School

TEN LITTLE BUGS

Ten little bugs
Sitting in a line,
One fell off
And then there were nine.

Nine little bugs
All went out,
One saw his mate
And then there were eight.

Eight little bugs
Went up to heaven,
One saw God
And then there were seven.

Seven little bugs
Playing with their sticks,
One lost his
And then there were six.

Six little bugs
Sitting in a hive,
One got stung
And then there were five.

Five little bugs
Rushing through the door,
One saw Mr Tozer
And then there were four.

Four little bugs
All had tea,
One had more
And then there were three.

Three little bugs
All went to the loo,
One fell down
And then there were two.

Two little bugs
All had some fun,
One had too much
And then there was one.

One little bug
Went out in the sun,
He got squashed
And then there were none.

Roxanne Ianson (11)
Parkwood Junior School

THROUGH THAT DOOR

Through that door,
A comet races above our heads,
Scattering the drifting clouds,
Racing to the sun.

Through that door,
An aeroplane crashes into the sea,
Drowning people surrounded by sharks,
Waiting for the midnight feast.

Through that door,
Two asteroids collide,
Mountains of dust falling to Earth,
Black hole sucking in the debris.

Ian Chambers & Nicholas Long (10)
Parkwood Junior School

ELEVEN GILLINGHAM FOOTBALLERS

Eleven Gillingham footballers,
Going to the den,
Ashby fails his fitness test
And then there were only ten.

Ten Gillingham footballers,
All the rest are fine,
Stevie Butler turns up late,
And now there are only nine.

Nine Gillingham footballers,
The fans are through the gate,
Millwall take the kick off,
And now there are only eight.

Eight Gillingham footballers,
Think that it is heaven,
Nicky Southall scores a goal,
And now there are only seven.

Seven Gillingham footballers,
Asaba doing tricks,
The crowd are going bonkers,
And now there are only six.

Six Gillingham footballers,
Paul Shaw takes a dive,
The referee points to the spot,
And now there are only five.

Five Gillingham footballers,
The penalty was poor,
It went straight at the keeper,
And now there are only four.

Four Gillingham footballers,
Butler hurts his knee,
He's carried off on a stretcher,
And now there are only three.

Three Gillingham footballers,
Pulis needs the loo,
He missed a bloomin' brilliant goal,
And now there are only two.

Two Gillingham footballers,
One cries for his mum,
His mother takes him away,
And now there is only one.

One Gillingham footballer,
Now his work is done,
Gillingham have won the league,
And now there are none.

Thomas Ball (11)
Parkwood Junior School

RATS!

Rats! Rats! Rats! They killed the cats
They fought the dogs
And ate cheeses from the vats.

They left fleas in our beds
Bit babies in cradles
Ate salted sprats from split open kegs.

Rats! Rats! They spoil women's chats
They left diseases in the kitchen
And made nests in men's best hats.

Rebecca Heale (11)
Parkwood Junior School

TEN PERFECT POEMS

Ten perfect poems
Looking at the time,
One looked too hard
And then there were nine.

Nine perfect poems
Found a perfect mate,
One got carried away
And then there were eight.

Eight perfect poems
Went up to heaven,
One met Elvis
And then there were seven.

Seven perfect poems
Playing with some tricks,
One did a disappearing act
And then there were six.

Six perfect poems
Playing with a hive,
One got stung to death
And then there were five.

Five perfect poems
Knocking on the door,
One got beaten up
And then there were four.

Four perfect poems
Playing by the sea,
One found a giant crab
And then there were three.

Three perfect poems
Went to the loo,
One got the door jammed
And then there were two.

Two perfect poems
Bathing in the sun,
One got sizzled up
And then there was one.

One perfect poem
Eating a bun,
He got stuck in jam
And then there was none.

So the perfect poems
Weren't so perfect
In the end . . . !

Jade Caccavone (10)
Parkwood Junior School

THE GAS BALL, JUPITER

The gas ball, Jupiter,
A colossal planet, largest of all,
Gigantic, fast-flying, rotating,
Like a ball of fire burning,
With a fiery core as red as ever.
It makes me feel as small as an ant,
Like a big foot's ready to stamp on me.
A gas ball, Jupiter.
It reminds me how Earth
Is compared to Jupiter.

Simon Lucas (10)
Parkwood Junior School

TEN MOULDY ALIENS

Ten mouldy aliens
Went to dine
One fell off the chair
And then there was nine.

Nine mouldy aliens
Walking out the gate
One drowned in the milk bottle
And then there were eight.

Eight mouldy aliens
Walking down to Devon
One walked off track
And then there were seven.

Seven mouldy aliens
Eating a double Twix
One floated right away
And then there were six.

Six mouldy aliens
Learning how to dive
One lost his swimming trunks
And then there were five.

Five mouldy aliens
Sitting on the floor
One got carpet burns
And then there were four.

Four mouldy aliens
Going for some tea
One got scalded bad
And then there were three.

Three mouldy aliens
Going to the loo
One got flushed away
And then there were two.

Two mouldy aliens
Sucking their thumbs
One sucked too hard
And then there was one.

One mouldy alien
Going to the sun
He got burnt to ashes
And then there were none.

Charlene Cotter (11)
Parkwood Junior School

WORLD WARS

World wars are not fun,
Especially when someone has a gun.
Why do people think it is a game,
They will not get any fame.

Bombs go *clang, clang!*
Fighters go *bang, bang!*

World wars are not fun,
Rubble falls by the ton.
Fighters fly in the sky,
The drop bombs, bye-bye!
Swoosh! Up I go, up the road.

Alex Forster (9)
Parkwood Junior School

JABBERWOCKY

It had just gone four in the afternoon,
When the sun was setting,
And when the misty smell had cleared
From the smelly room.
The Jabberwocky had just been meeting.

Beware the Jabberwocky my son!
The claws that bite, the claws that catch!
Beware the Jabberware or the shun,
The ones with the bad snatch.

He took his sword by the hand,
And for time the foe he sought -
Stood up by the yellow sand,
While lost in thought.

He thought he was finished as he stood,
The Jabberwocky with eyes of flame,
Came running through the small wood,
And wailed as it came.

One, two! One, two! he pulled out his lucky sword.
And the blade started to bang,
He left it dead and the eggs,
Then went galloping with a gang.

'It's the end of the Jabberwock,
Come to my arms boy!
What a wonderful day, hurrah! hurrah!'
And they shouted with joy.

It had just gone four in the afternoon,
When the sun was setting,
And when the misty smell had cleared
from the smelly room.
The Jabberwocky had just been melting.

Rhys Mant (10)
Parkwood Junior School

RATS

Rats, rats, they kill your cats,
They make nests in your Sunday hats.
They spread diseases
And they give out fleas.

I warn you, beware!

They bit the dogs
And hurt the babies in their cradles
And drink soup from the cooks' ladles.
Ate the cheese from the vats
And stopped the ladies' chats.

He got rid of the rats,
So they didn't kill the cats,
And they didn't spread diseases,
And they didn't give out fleas.

My thousand dollars, please,
Remember you owe me that
For I did kill the King Rat,
So he wouldn't hurt the babies in their cradles
And drink soup from the cooks' ladles.

Stacey Meaney (10)
Parkwood Junior School

TEN LITTLE PINK PIGS

Ten little pink pigs
Standing in a line,
One fell over,
And then there were nine.

Nine little pink pigs
Sitting on a gate,
One hopped off
And then there were eight.

Eight little pink pigs
Went up to heaven,
One went home
Then there were seven.

Seven little pink pigs
Picking up sticks,
One went away,
Then there were six.

Six little pink pigs
Near a hive,
One got stung,
Then there were five.

Five little pink pigs
Went through the door,
One fell over,
Then there were four.

Four little pink pigs
Chasing after me,
One tripped up and
Then there were three.

Three little pink pigs
All saying 'Boo',
One got frightened,
Then there were two.

Two little pink pigs
Out in the sun,
One got burnt,
Then there was one.

One little pink pig
Was having fun,
Then he went off
And then there was none.

Kizzy Ripley (11)
Parkwood Junior School

THROUGH THAT DOOR

Through that door
the midnight sky
glitters with the
roots of stars so beautiful,
in their silvery suits.

Through that door
is an unknown water world,
mermaids drifting by
with sparkling scales and
lifeless tails.

Through that door
is a wonder dream
of horses galloping through
a glimmering stream.

Anouska Lafferty & Lenna Rogers (11)
Parkwood Junior School

THE MAGIC BOX

I will put in the box,
Children's laughter as the waves splash against their legs,
The singing of a whale as she dances,
The gentle lapping of the calm, blue sea on the shore.

I will put in the box,
A snowman melting on to the grass,
A robin twittering to himself under a blanket of snow.

I will put in the box,
A witch flying on her broomstick across the moon,
A white, shiny tooth of a dragon as it bites its prey.

My box is styled with a flash of lightning and a floating Milky Way.
As you open the box, thunder roars.
The lock is made out of an eagle's beak.

I will swim in my box for miles and miles
until I find the British Isles.

Levi Courtney & Holly Preston (11)
Parkwood Junior School

SHARKS

Sharks, sharks everywhere,
They don't want to scare,
They want to tear.
They want to swim in deep ends
Because they want to meet new friends.

Sharks, sharks everywhere,
They don't want to lose their valuable hair.
They don't want fish swimming about
Because they want to scream and shout.

Zoe Porter (8)
Parkwood Junior School

CHILD LEFT BEHIND

Crippled kid left behind,
All his mates were not kind.
Sad and lonely, no playmates.
Stayed the same for loadsa dates.

        Poor little kid, he was jealous,
        Feeling ill, he was bilious.
        Miserable face, sad looking eyes,
        On a street, there he lies.

All in all, he was lonely,
He knew he was the one and only.
Left behind on an empty road,
On his own like a newborn child.

        Sobbing loudly, crying lots,
        He can imagine the other tots.
        Not very happy, sad today
        He cannot wait, to the next day.

Nick Bull (11)
Parkwood Junior School

EVACUATION

On the train I will go,
hard to believe,
suitcases next to me,
crying children all around me.

I miss the sound of my mother
calling for tea.
It feels like I'm all alone.
I still miss my friends, my family.

Carla Smith (10)
Parkwood Junior School

JABBERWOCKY

It was a misty and horrid day,
And the wind was moaning and groaning,
And the boats were bobbing in the bay,
As the Jabberwocky went that way.

Watch out! Watch out for that fiendish beast!
The claws that kill, the jaws of teeth.
Don't be scared just be brave
And take your sword to keep you safe.

As he rode on his horse,
he heard the beast a-coming.
He rode on in a different course,
The beast was ttt . . . turning.

He hid behind a mango tree, waiting for the beast.
As the monster came along,
He gave a sigh of relief,
He swung out with his sword with an almighty growl,

He shouted 'Yippee! Hooray!'
At the sight of the monster dead.
He got his long, sharp sword
And cut of the big, ugly head.

He picked it up and smiled,
then galloped back, shouting happily.

Shelley Rogers (11)
Parkwood Junior School

WORLD AT WAR

In the last world war,
people sometimes died.
Poppies grow in the fields
where the earth has risen.

Poppies turning red
in the setting sun.
People sadly crying
for people that are dead.

Debbie Thornton (11)
Parkwood Junior School

THE LONDON STREETS

'Whoah whoah' go the sirens,
'Quick get in' shouts our mum
'Bang bang' go the bombs
That's the Germans up above.

We were all sat down
Ready to cry,
We could hear the bombs
That was the scariest part.

We went back in just in case
I found it hard to sleep that night
Mother sneezing, so was I,
It was bad that night, I cried.

We were given the all clear
We went outside to see the streets,
Our house, yes you've guessed
It was bombed,
My mum let out an angry sigh.

My mum cried,
My dad sat down,
That's what the streets of London
Were like.

Grant Taylor (10)
Parkwood Junior School

MY PUPPY

She's nine weeks old.
She can catch cats' tails,
Barrel of fun,
Fun to play with,
She makes me happy,
She makes me want to play.
Cute, cuddly and lovely.

Alexis Ambler (11)
Parkwood Junior School

MONEY

Money, hard money,
Oh, bears buy honey with all their money.
No one spends money like my mummy,
Each time she goes shopping,
She buys good food for my tummy.
Yummy, yummy, yummy!

Joshua Short (9)
Parkwood Junior School

ADIDAS

A ll
D ay
I
D ream
A bout
S port.

Karl Choak (9)
Parkwood Junior School

JABBERWOCKY

It was a misty and horrid day
The wind was groaning and moaning
The Jabberwocky came along the bay
Jabberwocky came a moaning and groaning.

Beware the Jabberwocky my son!
The jaws that bite the claws that kill
Beware the monster that has always won
That's what it says in the book of will

He took his trusty sword in hand
To await the fearsome bread
By the old willow tree he did stand
To reflect upon his inevitable deed.

Behind the willow tree he stood
He had big round eyes of flame
He came through the wood sniffing and whiffing
And burbled as he came.

One two! One two! and through and through
He swung out sword with a wicker whack
He left it dead, and with his head
He went galloping back.

Oh well done my son! Oh well done
Oh come to my arms my brave boy
Oh fabulous day! Hip hip hooray!
He chortled in his joy.

It was a misty and horrid day
The wind was moaning and groaning
The Jabberwocky came along the bay
The Jabberwocky came a moaning and groaning.

Rohanna Clarke (11)
Parkwood Junior School

FIGHTING WARS 2000

World wars are not fun
When someone has a gun.
Sometimes you have to run,
Kill them,
Kill them.
Bombs explode,
They shake the road.
A bomb comes over,
It looks like a toad.
It can explode.
Kill them,
Kill them,
Bang!

Christopher Pritchard (8)
Parkwood Junior School

ADIDAS ALL DAY

A   ll
D   ay
I   'm
D   reaming
A   bout
S   wimming

A   t Splashes
L   ate at night.
L   ee is good at swimming,

D   anny is good at swimming,
A   dam is good at swimming,
Y   es, all of us are good at swimming.

Danny McDuell (9)
Parkwood Junior School

THE MAGIC BOX

I will put in the box,
The tongue of a Japanese fox,
The fearsome head of a Tyrannosaurus,
The tip of a pen touching papers as it writes.

I will put in the box,
A secret garden that glitters in the sun,
The foot of a crow, with a golden claw,
A snowflake from a winter's night.

I will put in the box,
The peachiness of a new-born baby's skin,
A never-ending rainbow, arching across the sky,
A single green scale from a mermaid's tail.

I will put in the box
The tip of a horn of a beautiful unicorn,
The silver haze of the stars shining down on Earth,
A comet shooting across the black sky.

My box is fashioned with sharks' teeth
Layered with gold and silver hair
Taken from a princess's head,
With snakes' eyes in the corners.

I shall fly in my box
With the spitfires,
With the birds and the sun.

Tara Dewey & Sarah Cobb (11)
Parkwood Junior School

RATS

Yo! Listen to my rap,
The rats are coming back,
They're carrying a disease,
Eating all the cheese,
So all beware,
Don't be scared.

They give us all fleas,
That's the disease,
So get on your knees
And beg the Pied Piper
To get the rats away
From our cheese.

So you've heard our rap,
The children got a smack,
And that's the end of our
rap about rats.

Sam Porter (11)
Parkwood Junior School

WAR

Germany invade Poland,
War is declared,
British and French get ready to attack,
Fighters in the sky.
German Messerschmidts, British Spitfires,
German U-boats, British subs.
Poppies in the fields
Where the men were killed,
Dog tags around their necks.

Paul Murthwaite-Price (11)
Parkwood Junior School

An Evacuee!

There hangs my gas mask,
I was trembling with fear,
Standing in a hall,
Waiting to be picked.
My suitcase on my right,
A girl on the left,
I felt alone,
Unloved.

I go to the country,
On a horse and cart
With an old lady.

I missed the busy hustle of people,
I missed the bombs, the screams,
Aeroplanes whizzing overhead,
And most of all my family,
Alone here in my head.

Katie Hales (10)
Parkwood Junior School

A Small Peabug

A small peabug,
Born days ago,
Tiny, wriggly, hard,
Like a stone in mud,
Like a scaly fish,
It makes me feel unnoticed,
Like a sea monkey's unknown.
A small peabug.
A small peabug out in the cold.

Lee Sycamore (11)
Parkwood Junior School

RATS

The rats fought the dogs and they killed the cats
And bit the babies in their cradles and ate the cheeses out of the vats,
They took soup from the cooks' own ladles.
They made nests in men's Sunday hats,
And even spoiled the women's chats.
They put germs all over the town.

The mayor thought that he would lose his job,
But the Pied Piper killed all the rats.
The mayor promised him 60,000 pounds, but broke his promise.
So the Piper promised to every child that he would
Take them to a fantastic place over the hill.
So they went, but one was left behind
Because he was too crippled.

Andrew McGowan (10)
Parkwood Junior School

SHARKS

Sharks swim fast and slow,
Sharks, sharks everywhere,
Sharks eat as they go,
Some big, some small,
Some dangerous, some not at all.
Some fat, some slim,
Sharks very deadly,
Some not at all.
Sharks very scary,
Some not at all.

Jonathan Maile (9)
Parkwood Junior School

RATS

The rats they nest in men's hats.
They fought the dogs
They killed the cats
They bit the babies
in their cradles.
They spread disease
They gave out fleas.

They ate the cheese,
They made people sneeze,
They drunk the soup,
They flew through a loop,
And they stopped the chats,
And they scared all the cats.

Lucy Hawes (11)
Parkwood Junior School

THE TINY HEDGEHOG

The tiny hedgehog
With a prickly back,
Scuffling, cute, wary,
Like a fir cone on the forest floor,
Like a bristle broom moving across the floor.
It makes me feel prickly and soft,
Like a conker shell lined with velvet.
The tiny hedgehog
Reminds me how
Beautiful nature really is.

Sally Buckle (11)
Parkwood Junior School

WAR! WAR! WAR!

One cold dark night
On the 5th November
1940 when I was born.

Bombed down houses,
People dead, guns going off
Bang! Bang!
Air raid wardens risking their lives
Air raid alarm going off.

Evacuees going to the country
I packed my bag
I had to walk to the countryside
Two weeks later my mum sent me
A telegraph to say my dad is dead
I wept and wept.

A year later more people were dead.
People wearing gas masks
Five years later the war ended
Hitler agreed to retreat
And peace fell on Earth.

Jonathan Reffell (10)
Parkwood Junior School

STARS

S   tars, stars, shining bright,
T   he stars shine bright in the night,
A   solar system high up there,
R   eally waiting to shine for a square.
S   tars, stars, shining bright.

Ashton Baylis (8)
Parkwood Junior School

THE PIED PIPER OF HAMLIN

It was morning and the rats did come,
Like an army with 1,000 men.
They charged into the town in groups
And ate up all the spaghetti hoops,
And then they started on the cheese
And ate up all the dairy.
The citizens of Hamlin were going bonkers
With the mayor. 'You'd better do something
About the rats because they're taking away our hats!'
'OK, OK,' said the mayor and swirled round on his chair.
And so the mayor went to Baler and saw the hippy man,
The Pied Piper, there.
He went on his knees and said 'Please,
Oh please, get rid of the fleas.
Get rid of the rats, get rid of the cats,
Get rid of the dogs, just get rid of everything!'
So the Piper did what he said,
But when he got there everyone was dead!

And the moral of this story is . . .
just go down to your supermarket and buy rat poison!

Matthew Peacock (11)
Parkwood Junior School

KELLY

K   is for Kelly, she is my friend.
E   is for Ellie, that is my fame name.
L   is for Leanne, nice and bright,
L   is for Lily, that is so silly.
Y   is for Yorick, that is a silly billy.

Ellie Owens (9)
Parkwood Junior School

BASHING CARS

Racing round in circles
and spinning round and round,
banging, crashing, banging,
trotting along and wrecking things.

Dominic Mason (8)
Parkwood Junior School

SPACE POEM

S   pacecraft go up from Earth,
P   eople and animals die,
A   dog called Laika died from lack of oxygen, the
C   raft was not designed to come back to
E   arth.

Joshua Peacock (8)
Parkwood Junior School

THE ALIEN

The alien slithered down the street,
Smelling just like cheesy feet.
His arms were swinging from side to side,
When I first saw him I nearly died.

Rebekah Ward (8)
Parkwood Junior School

WHAT IS WATER?

Water is a blue colouring pen,
Rapidly streaking across pale yellow paper.
It is a blueberry flavoured Slush Puppie,
When it melts, it sloshes across the cup.
It is blackcurrant flavoured Ribena,
Pouring into a glass.
It is a swimming pool for giants,
Sloshing over the sides.
It is the colour of blue,
Dripping from a white tap.

Matt Burrows (10)
Parkwood Junior School

THE RUMBLING VOLCANO

The rumbling volcano,
All made with lava,
Roaring, rumbling, shaking,
Like a diamond, dug half into the ground,
Like a treacle pudding with jam pouring out.
It makes me feel like eating it,
Like a lion on the prowl for its dinner.
The rumbling volcano,
Reminds us to beware!

Danielle Edwards (11)
Parkwood Junior School

THE JABBERWOCKY

Here he comes, big and old,
Covered in grease and lots of mould.
His big, white teeth chomp,
And his big feet stomp.

Jabberwocky, Jabberwocky, always beware,
With jaws that bite, and claws that catch,
Look out, you're in for a scare.
He hears a noise, his ears prick up.

A sword the seeker takes with him,
The Jabberwocky takes a swim,
The seeker sees and takes his aim . . .
The Jabberwocky knows his game.

Here he comes, big and old,
Covered in grease and lots of mould.
His big, white teeth chomp,
And his big feet stomp.

Kerry Nolan (11)
Parkwood Junior School

STAR

S   tar, star, sparkling at night.
T   hey twinkle in the night.
A   re they really sparkling?
R   eally, are they so bright in the night?

Leanne Curtis (8)
Parkwood Junior School

JABBERWOCKY

It was blinding and had a snake-like tail,
It trampled along and how it did slither.
It was slimy and had a back like a sail,
But when you see it, oh how you will quiver.

'Beware of the Jabberwock my son, be brave.'
The jaws that bite and the claws that catch.
'Look, there he goes quickly in that cave.'
It was gloomy and dark, it was.

A foolish boy he did approach,
And gobbled him up he did.
He swaggered along in a contented way,
Prey he was no longer yearning.

A boy then shot the dragon
And so he dropped down dead.
His eyes of flame then turned to stone
And the boy he took his head.

Kayleigh Slattery (11)
Parkwood Junior School

SPACE

S   pace is very dark,
P   eople leave their mark,
A   nd then they go to Earth,
C   ause then they blast to Perth.
E   verywhere is black and dark.

Callum Essam (9)
Parkwood Junior School

THE MAGIC BOX

I will put in the box,
The swish of a unicorn's tail,
A flash of the sun on a summer's day,
The sparkling of a star's ray, glittering down to earth.

I will put in the box,
The sound of a bee quietly humming in a field,
The note from a nightingale,
A slither of ice from Saturn's ring.

I will put in the box,
The green glow of a cat's eye,
The tinkling of a bell from a tag round an eagle's talon,
The ripple of water as the mallard swims by.

I will put in the box,
The magic of a four-leaf clover,
A frosty strand from the unicorn's mane,
The sun setting over the blue ocean below the cliffs.

I will put in the box,
The scuffling of a mole digging its way through the earth,
A drop of golden sun,
The power of an alligator's jaw,
And a glistening drop of dew.

My box has a lock of a golden dragon's claw.
On the lid, it has pictures of dragons and unicorns.
The corners of the box are made of bits of rainbow.
Surrounding the lock is the Milky Way in front of the
                                    gold box.

Nicola Cartledge (10)
Parkwood Junior School

MY CAT, SMUDGE

This lonely fellow
Was quite a cello,
With one hair on his cheek.
He was very small,
With smallest eyes,
With flowing tears
Which made me cry.

We picked him up,
And washed him clean,
Then all at once came back with fear.
We wiped him down
And washed his eyes,
And all at once he started to lie down.

Then David's Dad came over
And said,
'He's quite like a stripy wall in bed.'
We called him Smudge,
So that's his name.

Now he's ours, he's quite like you,
And like a Gooner running,
He runs around,
Giving a shout,
And jumps on shoulders and sleeps on you,
Like a tiny, little bug.

He won't let us go outside.
He'll just sit on your knee,
He is loved and cared for.
So that's the life of little Smudge.

Matthew Thomas (10)
Parkwood Junior School

JABBERWOCKY

It was afternoon and the mist swirled round,
The trees swayed in the breeze,
The mud was piled in tall, thick mounds
And low were the branches of the willow trees.

Beware the Jabberwocky, my son!
From behind a tree, bush or dainty flower,
With jaws that bite and claws that catch,
Will come the Jabberwocky with terrible power.

In his hand, he did hold his sword,
A wait he had to slay this beast,
Behind a tree with sweet green peas.
The Jabberwocky, did he smell the scent of fresh English blood?

Following the lovely scent of English blood
The Jabberwocky comes. He comes from
The overgrown wood, the beast with
The long, black, greasy mane.

From behind the tree, the slayer did jump
To kill, to slay the Jabberwocky.
The slayer did leave him dead,
And went heavily plodding back with his head.

It was afternoon and the mist swirled round,
The trees swayed in the breeze.
The mud was piled in tall, thick mounds,
And low were the branches of the willow trees.

Carly Elphick (11)
Parkwood Junior School

JABBERWOCKY

It started in the afternoon,
It did at four o'clock.
The sun was shining in the middle of June,
They were scared of the Jabberwock.

'Beware the Jabberwock, my son!'
The jaws that bite, the claws that catch,
The Jabberwock does not give a sign of fun,
So beware, he will scratch.

So he took off to the Jabberwock,
With a sword in his pocket,
Dressed in armour from head to sock,
He went to fight the Jabberwock.

The boy arrived to fight the dragon
And pulled his sword from his pocket,
And hit the dragon into a lagoon
And pushed it down a hill.

And so he killed the Jabberwock,
His dad chortled in joy.
'Oh fabulous day, hip, hip hooray.
Congratulations my boy.'

It started in the afternoon,
It did at four o'clock.
The sun was shining in the middle of June,
They were scared of the Jabberwock.

Daniel Triplow (11)
Parkwood Junior School

THE PALE MOON

The pale moon
With six times less gravity than us.
Desolate, lonely, fascinating,
Like a silver ball hanging in space.
Like a dusty desert
It makes me feel calm and sleepy,
Like a dormouse curling up in the warmth.
The pale moon
Reminds me of how precious life is.

Sarah Buchanan (10)
Parkwood Junior School

MILLENNIUM

Millennium is such a treat,
So everybody take your seat.

Millennium is coming soon,
Just watch the rise of the moon.

Millennium has its own dome,
Inside which you can roam.

Millennium has a computer bug,
Although it's nothing like a garden slug.

So just wait another year or so,
And the weeks and the days will start to go,
Then at twelve o'clock you'll hear a cheer
'Hooray,' 'Hooray.'
The millennium's here.

Zoe Etheridge (11)
St Benedict's RC Primary School, Chatham

MILLENNIUM

The new year to me
Is like a nice cup of tea,
You can start all over,
And then you'll never fall over,
It'll probably make me feel strong and brave,
And so I'll be likely to see the ocean wave.
To have a new year I'll feel very glad
And not at all sad.
I'll be sad for the year to go by, 1999
But it's just like starting a fresh new line.
The year 2000 will be new for me
As I'm waiting for the count of three.
I'll say goodbye another time
As I'm trying to make this poem rhyme.
Everyone will get excited
But they'll probably still shout 'Man United'
As I'm just waiting for the millennium.

Karen Gordon (11)
St Benedict's RC Primary School, Chatham

MILLENNIUM

The millennium is approaching fast,
It's coming round the corner with a blast,
With the computer bug and the global warming,
Everyone celebrating the New Year with a bang,
All the parents laughing and joking,
Kids and babies running around,
And everyone celebrating in the town.

Jemma Collins (10)
St Benedict's RC Primary School, Chatham

MILLENNIUM

Would I build a Millennium Dome
Or would I help the homeless?
Would I build a Millennium Dome
Or would I feed the poor?

Would I build a Millennium Dome
Or would I help the disabled?
Would I build a Millennium Dome
Or would I help those in need?

Would I build a Millennium Dome
Or would I help those dying?
Would I build a Millennium Dome
Or would I help to bring peace?

Would I build a Millennium Dome
Or would I build a church to unite the nation?
Would I build a Millennium Dome
Or would I help the buildings that need it?

I only wish they'd thought about it more!

Peter Vik (10)
St Benedict's RC Primary School, Chatham

THE MILLENNIUM

The millennium is the beginning of the new next century,
Where we'll all be celebrating 2000 years.
There's only 326 days to go, they've even built a dome.
To show that we know.

There will be lots of parties in 1999.
To see the millennium in and have a good time.
It's celebrating 2000 years after Jesus Christ's birth
To show we believe in him after he left.

2000 years is a long long time.
The world has changed well down the line.
Hopefully his star will shine.

The Earth is changing day by day.
We learn to adapt along the way.
So here is the millennium on its way.

Luke Thorne (11)
St Benedict's RC Primary School, Chatham

MILLENNIUM

The millennium comes once in a lifetime,
Sitting on a fence.
Waiting to be opened,
So let's all seek.

Whooo
I've found it,
Here it comes.
Another few minutes,
Bang boom it's all
Done.

See
You
Next time,
I can't
Wait to see.
Fireworks
Will be
Banging
All over the
Sea.

Michelle Barton (11)
St Benedict's RC Primary School, Chatham

MILLENNIUM

No need to carry things around,
A pair of Hoover hands can be found.
When you drive somewhere, you go kind of slow,
But type in the area and off you go.
TVs are now not what they seem,
'Cause everyone comes with a portable TV screen.
No going to school, no more class sessions,
Because now there is a TV with the same subject lessons.
Being afraid of the dark is never a worry,
They're putting mirrors on the moon, but not in a hurry.
Not the same people in the hall of fame,
But apart from that, everything's the same!

Gary Crawford (10)
St Benedict's RC Primary School, Chatham

MILLENNIUM

The millennium is coming
At the end of this year
The year 2000
Let's hear a cheer
A party we will share
With our friends from the year
Goodbye 1990s
We are sorry to leave you
Hello year 2000
We are happy to see you.

Martin McDaid (11)
St Benedict's RC Primary School, Chatham

THE YEAR 2000

I think in the year 2000
People will try hard
To take care of the world
And everything in it, and that's alive
That's what I think.

Make the world a better place
Maybe they will protect
The animals and not kill
Them and each other
That's what I think.

The year 2000 will
Be great, superb
In fact I know
Well actually
That's only what I think.

Anneliese Clare D'Souza (11)
St Benedict's RC Primary School, Chatham

MILLENNIUM

Millennium is the time of joy
It makes you jump twist and turn
That I would start to burn
I would feel so great
Instead of being in a real state

The millennium is coming soon
And so is the moon
When the moon comes out
The millennium is all I dream about.

Leanne Ferguson (11)
St Benedict's RC Primary School, Chatham

MILLENNIUM

I wonder what the fuss is about,
Everyone wants to shout,
'Millennium, millennium'
That's what they want to say
In one ear and out the other.

Millennium, millennium,
Makes me want to scream,
What is the millennium,
It's joy it's peace,
Can't you believe.

Now I know why people
Are going nuts.
Whoa, let me go
Into the millennium,
That's what the fuss is about.

Amy Caulfield (1)
St Benedict's RC Primary School, Chatham

MILLENNIUM

With the dome stadium
Being built for the millennium
As each day of 1999 that passes
We get closer to the biggest party.
There will be dancing and
singing in the streets
To celebrate this unique feat
This will only happen once in our lifetime
So let us all have a good time.

Lauren Parsons (11)
St Benedict's RC Primary School, Chatham

MILLENNIUM

Millennium what a special time,
It will only happen once in my lifetime.
A thousand years have passed us by,
A dome is planned to reach the sky.
A party is what we have planned,
With family and friends from different lands.
Most will travel far and wide,
To be at our side.
Party poppers, food and drink,
Music, dancing will make us think.
Of times gone by,
And times to come.
I hope this millennium will,
Be a special one.
Millennium what a special time,
It will happen once in my lifetime.

Oliver Robert Barnard (10)
St Benedict's RC Primary School, Chatham

SAD OR HAPPY - MILLENNIUM 2000

What would happen in the millennium 2000?
What will happen?
Will it be happy?
Will it be sad
Or might it be the worst thing?
Very very bad?
But what will happen?
What will?
I wish it was going to be happy days
Hopefully not crowded days with the bill.

Laura Simpson (11)
St Benedict's RC Primary School, Chatham

THE YEAR 2000

Oh love and care
It will be everywhere
Peace not war
A 50-50 score
There will be lots more
And we will have new
things to satisfy us through
Our lives till the day
We will pass away
With our very happy souls.

Jason Gary Evatt (11)
St Benedict's RC Primary School, Chatham

A MARVELLOUS MILLENNIUM

The millennium's going to be stunning,
vivacious, exuberant and bright.
At millennium dogs'll be running,
away from the raucous noises and the vivid light.

Havoc at the hospitals, with new millennium,
and the effects of the Millennium Bug.
There'll be lots of fearful maybes,
when passed by a drunken thug.

But millennium won't be that bad,
there will be loads of parties,
where people will go absolutely *mad,*
and children'll swallow whole Smarties.

Adults and children giggling and dancing,
parents and youngsters smiling and prancing.

Emma Parrick (11)
St Botolph's CEP School, Northfleet

MILLENNIUM

We can't wait until the millennium
In the pubs it will be pandemonium
And everyone gets in a panic
When there is an hour of work to go.

With all the parties everyone is happy
And all the grownups are chappy
With all the fireworks going off
All the noise is going on.

I can't wait until the millennium.

We can't wait until the big big *big*
Dome opens I'll be at home eating a fig
Hopefully my family will go to it
Eating all the food and drink makes me happy
I really can't wait until the
Millennium.

Mark Blowers (11)
St Botolph's CEP School, Northfleet

MILLENNIUM BUG

The Millennium Bug has a nice journey to the computer,
has a ride on a disc for a lift
and if you are lucky the Millennium Bug
                    might turn up on your telly.

The Millennium Bug, the Millennium Bug,
the Millennium Bug is coming.
You don't know when it will strike again
that is probably when you're twenty.

Charlotte Parks (10)
St Botolph's CEP School, Northfleet

Fireworks

Fireworks here,
fireworks there.
Fireworks are
everywhere.

Frightful explosions
which burst your ears.

'Look at the big one,'
says the kid, tugging at my sleeve.

As the millennium
draws closer
the noise gets louder.
Then at long last
comes the big,
big *bang!*

Then we're
in a new century.

Dominic Barnes (10)
St Botolph's CEP School, Northfleet

The Millennium Year

I can't wait the Millennium's coming,
Parties, drink and all.
Everybody celebrating with friends,
Excited, cheerful and thrills everywhere.

I want a party, invite everyone.
Lights right round my house
And decorations all over.
Maybe even gifts will be given and received.

Fireworks and lights,
Extraordinary and colourful.
Ships with flares and foghorns,
Dazzling and gleaming everywhere.

New buildings will be built
Like the Millennium Dome.
Prices will go up and
New happenings will be created.
I just can't wait!

Katy Heasman (11)
St Botolph's CEP School, Northfleet

CELEBRATION 2000

Millennium millennium
You are a bug
Leave our computers alone.

Millennium millennium
You're the year's bully
Leave our computers alone.

Millennium millennium
You cause all the problems
Leave our computers alone.

Millennium millennium
You are the year's problems
Leave our computers alone.

Millennium millennium
We'll be happy when you're gone
Will poorer countries notice?

Bradley Jarrett (10)
St Botolph's CEP School, Northfleet

MILLENNIUM

When the year two thousand comes,
will people put on weight so they weigh tons?
Will there be parties? I think there should.
In the Millennium Dome will there be sculptures
                                        made out of wood?

Will there be fireworks that go, *bang, bang, bang*?
And will there be drinks that give you a tang?
Will the Millennium Bug actually exist?
And will computers go round the twist?

Will there be party poppers that fire coloured strings
and will we get some very nice things?
Will people get drunk while they're on the booze,
then at the end will they have a nice long snooze?

At twelve o'clock will people shout, 'It's the *millennium!*'

Hannah Siggers (9)
St Botolph's CEP School, Northfleet

CELEBRATION 2000

The parties will be great
in the year 2000
The parties in the Dome
The parties in our homes
The parties down our roads.

Will the Dome be built?
Will we be able to visit?
We just don't know
Till we're there.

Leslie Barrass (11)
St Botolph's CEP School, Northfleet

CELEBRATION 2000

Celebrations
Here they come
Running up the time line.

Year 2000
It is here
We're all gonna
Cheer and cheer.

Dancing, partying
Eating food
We're all boisterous
As can be.

Jodi Laura Parmenter (11)
St Botolph's CEP School, Northfleet

THE MILLENNIUM

The bug will be the
bad part of the millennium.
There are going to be fallouts
with computers and electric
because of it.

The parties are going to be big
the raves are to be great.
There are going to be fireworks everywhere.

The Millennium Dome
will be packed with excitement
and fun things for adults, teenagers and children.

Jennifer Moule (9)
St Botolph's CEP School, Northfleet

CELEBRATION 2000

Parties here! Parties there!
The millennium is near
The future is clear
Cocktail, wine, beer
Champagne
Refreshment, food it's all the same
It's just the start of the New Year again
In the house or in the pub
They all shout at 12 o'clock
In the year 2001
They'll shout just as much
Time shall go on.

Daniel Dadwal (11)
St Botolph's CEP School, Northfleet

CELEBRATION 2000

T oo long we have waited for the year 2000
W onderful as it is
O h no the computers are going to crash down on us

T ime to party people
H opefully we'll have fun
O h the millennium is coming. Beware of the bug
U ntil the time is over, enjoy the time you have
S tock up with food before it comes
A nd then we will be able to laugh all night
N ow we're going to cheer and cheer
D ance, eat and drink away.

Krystal Burton-Grey (10)
St Botolph's CEP School, Northfleet

PARTY TIME 2000

Soon the time will come,
To have a lot of fun.
When the clock strikes midnight,
The sky will be bright,
Full of vivid colours.

The millennium is full of fun,
People can't wait for it to come.
Dancing in the night,
The sky so light,
Full of lively colours.

Soon it will be party time,
Fireworks red, blue and lime,
Gold, silver, green all in different places.
Smiles on everyone's faces,
Because it's the *millennium!*

Kerry Reilly (11)
St Botolph's CEP School, Northfleet

CELEBRATION 2000

M illennium is coming
I   t's going to be so merry, twelve midnight strikes
L   oads of people sing and dance
L   ots of colours in the sky
E   veryone is so amazed
N ot every year is so incredible
N ew is the year, old is 1999
I   think this year is the best
U nusual will be the year to come
M achines are being invented everywhere.

Kevin Parrick (9)
St Botolph's CEP School, Northfleet

CELEBRATION 2000

C atherine wheels sparkling.
E verybody having a cheerful time.
L aughter and happiness.
E xcited people having a joyful time.
B ang goes a firework.
R elaxation for the parents.
A lively party.
T errific party poppers going everywhere.
I ncredible fireworks.
O rganised people having a laugh.
N obody terrified about the Millennium Bug.

2 000 what a big number.
0 verjoyed people getting drunk.
0 ut and about people are celebrating.
0 h no, the food's got burnt.

Katie Archer (11)
St Botolph's CEP School, Northfleet

CELEBRATION 2000

Year 2000 is coming soon
Everyone's excited
Fireworks will be reaching the moon
Everyone's delighted.

Celebrations are everywhere
Decorations in every house
Parties here and parties there
Everyone will be celebrating, even the mouse

But will everyone be celebrating?

Anna Chan (11)
St Botolph's CEP School, Northfleet

CELEBRATION 2000

Millennium! Who knows what's coming?
Computers might crash
or celebrations
it may be happy
or not at all.
What's a Millennium Bug?

Will it invade
it might
who knows?
I hope not
it might infect mobile phones
my dad's got one
it had better not
otherwise
I won't hear from him.

Stephen Bage (9)
St Botolph's CEP School, Northfleet

CELEBRATION 2000

M illennium is coming soon,
I t will come at midnight,
L eaping on us like a lion in the dark
L etting everyone know
E nd of the year 1999
N ow I wish I was invisible
N ew year's everywhere
I hope we have lots of parties
U nder all the fireworks
M illennium is coming soon.

Louise Fielder-White (10)
St Botolph's CEP School, Northfleet

CELEBRATION 2000

Party balloons covered the house,
Plenty of food and drink,
Crackers and party poppers ready to explode,
Fluorescent fireworks bright pink.
I'm waiting for the crowd to arrive,
The waiting seems like weeks!

Here they come, 400 stamping feet,
They've gobbled down the food,
The crackers go bang, the poppers pop,
With a spray of confetti,
We dance till we drop!

The parcel is passed,
The drink is drunk,
A millennium is finished and another has a start.

Kayleigh-Anne Soryal (10)
St Botolph's CEP School, Northfleet

MILLENNIUM BUG

Millennium Bug, Millennium Bug,
The Millennium Bug is coming.
What will happen to computers?
Crimes and dangers on the way.
The Millennium Bug is coming.

But let's try to forget, yes forget.
The Millennium Bug is coming.
We have still got time to forget.
Let's party and celebrate and forget.
The Millennium Bug is coming.

Hannah Payne (9)
St Botolph's CEP School, Northfleet

CELEBRATION 2000

T he time has nearly come,
H ear the noises that are around.
E x.citement, excitement we'll hear soon.

M onstrous for some people.
I llness for computers it might be.
L olloping happily around the street,
L olloping happily around everyone.
E xciting it might be
N ot very funny people might think,
N ot very funny people might say.
I n and out of places, happily.
U ntil it's the year 2001,
M illennium it will be.

Carlie Warren (11)
St Botolph's CEP School, Northfleet

CELEBRATION 2000

The year 2000 is closing fast
Time to think of the future, not the past
Having parties, loads of fun
It's time to celebrate, everyone.

The millennium is nearly here
Nobody can wait for the New Year
Even more parties, even more fun
I bet you can't wait
For the New Year to come.

Rebecca Hall (11)
St Botolph's CEP School, Northfleet

MILLENNIUM

The millennium will be joyful and exciting.
There's going to be fantastic fun fireworks.
Fireworks, noisy, colourful and amazing,
Whizzing, twirling and whirling about.
Everyone's going to be happy and joyful.
While I'll be going over the moon!

People dancing,
Singing and prancing.
I'll be popping party poppers,
pop, pop, pop!

Parties with millions of lights,
People will have loads of frights.
In the year 2000
The millennium is going to be joyful and exciting.

Laura Chan (9)
St Botolph's CEP School, Northfleet

CELEBRATION 2000

Lots of lights
which are very bright,
all in one night.
Everyone is really joyful,
not to mention very lively.
Lots of parties, lots of fireworks *errkk!*
Look there's a man called Mick.
Cor blimey, I feel sick.
Don't you?

Jason Bright (9)
St Botolph's CEP School, Northfleet

CELEBRATION 2000

The year 2000 is nearly here
I cannot wait till the new year
Parties galore people lying drunk on the floor
I've never seen as much excitement as this before

Millennium here millennium there
You heard, I heard about that
But I'll tell you what

Open parties for everyone
Beer and laughter
Until the final countdown
10, 9, 8, 7, 6, 5, 4, 3, 2, 1
Then what . . .

Zoe Blowers (11)
St Botolph's CEP School, Northfleet

ATTRACTIONS 2000

Firstly I'll go to the Millennium Dome
Afterwards I'll go back home
I'll get there on the Jubilee track
Then I'll shut the door with a great big whack!
I'll be excited
Because the fireworks will be brightly lighted
With lots of multi-coloured lights
This will be the most amazing of sights!
All the streets will be busy,
People walking till they all get dizzy!
My face won't be a look of dismay
Because the new millennium will be a wonderful day!

Philip Beech (9)
St Botolph's CEP School, Northfleet

MILLENNIUM

Flashing lights,
Real loud music,
People in crowds,
Dancing to the music.

Fireworks whizzing,
In all different ways,
All the bright colours,
Makes everyone gaze.

Everybody is excited,
Everybody's amazed,
Everybody's talking and laughing,
Everybody's entertained.

Jamie Davies (10)
St Botolph's CEP School, Northfleet

2000

The 2000, so exciting!
With lots of lights and parties.
Shouts, yells, screams and roars of laughter and joy.
There's going to be excitement, music, presents
and the countdown.

Fireworks are the best though,
being amazing, colourful, bright and stunning
as they whizz through the air.
London is going to be busy,
But hopefully everyone will forget about
the Millennium Bug!

Aran Wade (9)
St Botolph's CEP School, Northfleet

CELEBRATION 2000

The big 2000 is almost here,
Party time is coming,
Balloons are being blown up,
And the Dome is going to be finished.

But will we be partying?
Will the bug get us?
Will it kill our computers
Or will we be safe?

Will planes fall from the sky,
And crash land in our gardens?
Will we have a great new year?
Will we be safe?

Carly Dickman (11)
St Botolph's CEP School, Northfleet

CELEBRATION 2000

The year 2000 is coming fast
Time to think about future not past
'We're having a party everyone
Come and join in the fun.'

The millennium is coming soon
Even more parties even more balloons
Even more people even more fun
Time to celebrate everyone.

Party here party there
Stop lazing about in that chair
Keep on dancing everyone
We need to have a lot of fun.

Clare Oliver (9)
St Botolph's CEP School, Northfleet

CELEBRATION 2000

Lots of lights,
fireworks so bright.
Parties all around,
really big sounds.

The Millennium Bug,
as cosy as a rug.
In our computers,
destroying the future.

Everybody happy,
everybody wacky,
and everybody celebrating the millennium.

James Willis (11)
St Botolph's CEP School, Northfleet

CELEBRATION 2000

C elebrate the year 2000
E veryone roaring, screaming
L aughing for the new year
E asy come, easy go thousands
B ang from the fireworks in the sky
R obbie Williams plays Millennium
A nd make your new year resolutions now
T he children excited
I t's going to be brilliant
O n 10, 9, 8, 7, 6, 5, 4, 3, 2, 1
N ow celebrate!

Kallie M Heap (10)
St Botolph's CEP School, Northfleet

CELEBRATION 2000

Will there be a Millennium Dome?
Will there be computers?
Will we ever know?

If there is a Millennium Dome
If there are computers
Will we be happier than ever?
We don't really know!

Christine Martin (10)
St Botolph's CEP School, Northfleet

CELEBRATION 2000

There's a Millennium Bug,
So give your computer a hug,

There's going to be a jam,
So go help your gran,

All the computers will crash,
So give your aunty a bash.

James Payne (11)
St Botolph's CEP School, Northfleet

MARY HAD A ROBOT LAMB

Mary had a little lamb, she went to the shop
and the butcher said, 'It's got the Millennium Bug.'
The butcher said, 'Get down, it's going to blow up.
Now go to the Millennium Dome and get a new one
and go and celebrate the millennium 2000!'

Tarren Sharp (10)
St Botolph's CEP School, Northfleet

CELEBRATION 2000

Celebrations it is supposed to be but,
The *bug* is here,
'There's lots of trouble
in the air,'
Shout the pilots of the planes.
The people of this land are suffering,
BT shut down and so do The BBC.
Nobody can defeat this evil age.

Ross Maynard (10)
St Botolph's CEP School, Northfleet

MILLENNIUM

Millennium, millennium, joyful millennium.
Fireworks, fireworks, sparkling fireworks.
Parties, parties, exciting parties.
Babies, babies, yelling babies!
Millennium Bug, Millennium Bug, aggravating everyone.

Millennium, millennium, here at last.
Millennium, millennium, hip, hip hooray.

Shirell Spicer (10)
St Botolph's CEP School, Northfleet

CELEBRATION 2000

Celebration is a box of chocolates.
You think they are going to be nice,
But you're not sure.
They might be beautiful or horrible.

Tony Barham (11)
St Botolph's CEP School, Northfleet

SEASONS OF THE YEAR

Summer

Summer is here now
Children playing on the pier
Watching boats go by.

Winter

Winter's here again
Like the first season ever
Cats sleep by the fire.

Autumn

Autumn is here with
Rotting leaves falling off trees.
Like last year's autumn.

Spring

The spring is starting
The flowers are growing now
Sheep are being born.

Sam Isaacs (10)
St Helen's CE Primary School, Cliffe

A SUNNY DAY

Listen
you can hear birds,
you have lots of ice-cream.
Children play outside happily,
happy.

Megan Jeffrey (10)
St Helen's CE Primary School, Cliffe

SEASONS

Winter

Sun goes and snow comes.
Days are getting very dark.
It is very cold.

Spring

Animals are born.
The plants start to grow again.
It starts to get hot.

Summer

The nights are lighter.
Kids go on the beach to swim.
The sun gets hotter.

Autumn

The leaves start to fall.
The days are even shorter.
The plants start to die.

Sarah Ebbs (10)
St Helen's CE Primary School, Cliffe

SUMMER DAYS

Sshh! Wait
birds are coming.
Listen, hear them sing songs.
Sweet songs for you and the whole world.
Lovely.

Dean Ellis (10)
St Helen's CE Primary School, Cliffe

HAIKU SEASONS

Autumn

The child runs around.
The trees get twiggy and bear.
The child stares around.

Spring

The trees start to bud.
The children pick some flowers.
It starts all again.

Summer

Summer is quite hot.
Leaves start to awaken again.
Summer has come back.

Winter

Winter's always cold.
You have to have some booties.
Winter's quite funny.

Samantha Louise Mitchell (10)
St Helen's CE Primary School, Cliffe

A HORSE AND A FLEA

A horse and a flea and three blind mice,
sat on a kerbstone shooting dice.
The horse slipped and fell on the flea.
The flea said, 'Whoops, there's a horse on me.'

Hannah Loveridge (11)
St Helen's CE Primary School, Cliffe

SEASONS HAIKU

Summer

Summer is not cold.
Flowers are grown by the sun.
It burns you a lot.

Winter

Winter is freezing.
Winter has snow and has frost.
You need woolly hats.

Spring

Leaves grow green again.
Trees are very happy things.
Spring is Easter Day.

Autumn

In autumn it's fresh
Autumn is when leaves fall off
and the nights draw in.

Lewis Rixson (11)
St Helen's CE Primary School, Cliffe

WINTER NIGHT

Listen.
Hear the snow crunch
like big feet passing.
All leaves are like icicles falling.
Listen.

Kayleigh Herbert (11)
St Helen's CE Primary School, Cliffe

HAIKU

Autumn

The days get shorter.
Leaves start to fall and change to brown.
The night falls quicker.

Spring

Flowers start to grow.
Lambs are starting to be born.
Blossom starts to form.

Summer

You start to chill out.
The days start to get longer.
We all eat ice-cream.

Winter

The days get colder.
It is very slippery outside.
It is now snowing.

Maxine Shaw (10)
St Helen's CE Primary School, Cliffe

OUR SCHOOL

'Our school is a lot of help,' say the girls tidying up.
'Our school is kind,' say the children helping others up.
'Our school makes a lot of friends,' say the teachers with smiles.
'Our school is a fantastic place,' say the whirring computers in white.
'Our school is a fabulous place,' say the children working.

Ashleigh Ahkin (8)
St Helen's CE Primary School, Cliffe

Quietly

Quietly, the ocean splashes me.
Quietly, the tooth fairy gets my tooth from my pillow.
Quietly, the bees and birds hum.
Quietly, I play babies.
Quietly, I pat a dog.
Quietly, the kids' feet sink in the sand.
Quietly, I drink happily.
Quietly, I go on my horse.
Quietly, my horse trots to my house.
Quietly, I cuddle my mum and dad.
Quietly, I go to sleep.
Quietly, the car goes in a rush.
Quietly the bears snuggle up to their mums.

Jessica Springhall (8)
St Helen's CE Primary School, Cliffe

Our School

'Our school is a making school,'
say the scissors and paper.

'Our school is a noisy school,'
say the banging cupboards.

'Our school is a clean school,'
say the mops and buckets of water.

'Our school is a writing school,'
say the pens and pencils.

Ben Blackman (8)
St Helen's CE Primary School, Cliffe

OUR SCHOOL

'Our school is a clean and tidy place,' say the polished chairs and high tables and the sparkling floor.

'Our school is a joyful place,' say the green grass, the tidy books and the bouncy pillows.

'Our school is a noisy place,' say the light-pink walls, the dusty doors and the good displays.

'Our school is a happy place,' say the dancing flowers and chalky blackboards.

'Our school is a truthful place,' say the children telling the truth and being fair.

Hollie Slater (8)
St Helen's CE Primary School, Cliffe

OUR SCHOOL

'Our school is a clean and posh school,' say the teachers in make up, kids working hard and the headmaster telling me off!

'Our school is a loving school,' say kids on the playground sharing their toys, teacher's caring.

'Our school is a giant and colourful school,' say the sparkling books and shiny floors and the posh windows.

'Our school is a sparkling school,' say the plush carpets, neat displays, printing computers and hard-working kids.

'Our school is a clever school,' say the finished work, the sharp pens and pencils and standing books.

Lauren Medcraft (8)
St Helen's CE Primary School, Cliffe

ANIMAL MASQUERADE

Bet you didn't know
a log could start to walk around
and swim right up to you.
That's me a crocodile.

Bet you didn't know
a tree stump could start to roar
and howl in the wind.
That's starving old me, a bear.

Bet you didn't know
a snowball could start to hop
and skip around the street.
That's white old me, a hare.

Alex Turner (8)
St Helen's CE Primary School, Cliffe

ANIMAL MASQUERADE

Bet you didn't know a zebra cross could walk
Because I'm a zebra.

Bet you didn't know a flower could fly
Because I'm a butterfly.

Bet you didn't know a leaf could hop
Because I'm a grasshopper.

Bet you didn't know a leaf could hop
Because I'm a toad.

Lucy Henrick (8)
St Helen's CE Primary School, Cliffe

OUR SCHOOL

'Our school is a busy place,'
say the clonking shoes
and lines of children.

'Our school is a quiet place,'
say the children working
and teachers marking work.

'Our school is a working place,'
say the happy pencils
and beautiful work on the displays.

'Our school is a proud place,'
say the school rules
and the smiling books.

'Our school is a polite place,'
say the walking children
and the children with hands in the air.

Maria Richards (8)
St Helen's CE Primary School, Cliffe

SOFTLY

Softly I tiptoed across the path,
Softly I ran across the damp grass.
Softly we painted my bedroom wall,
Softly the robber crept across the hall.

Softly I breathe in my cosy bed,
Softly a feather lands on my head.
Softly the wind runs through my hair,
Softly I climb up the stair.

Oliver Theobald (8)
St Helen's CE Primary School, Cliffe

OUR SCHOOL

'Our school is not a scruffy place,'
say the neat displays, shining baskets
and the giggling poetry books.

'Our school is a joyful place,'
says the dancing PE equipment,
dancing pencils and opening books.

'Our school is a tidy place,'
say the polished tables, clean chairs and sharp pencils.

'Our school has lots of kind people,'
say the helpful children, happy faces
and dancing children.

'Our school is very colourful,'
say the backgrounds and the sparkling work
and the shiny pens.

Ellie Pigden (9)
St Helen's CE Primary School, Cliffe

LIGHTLY

Lightly the bee buzzes round the park.
Lightly the ladybird crosses a leaf.
Lightly the clouds slowly spin.
Lightly the flag blows through the mid air.
Lightly the rain falls on the rooftops.
Lightly the feathers drop from the nest.
Lightly the trees rustle.
Lightly the fairies tiptoe across the roof.
Lightly the light flies are buzzing around.
Lightly the street lamps flicker on.

Charlee Jeffrey (8)
St Helen's CE Primary School, Cliffe

OUR SCHOOL

'Our school is a clean place,'
say the bins full of rubbish,
the pencil sharpener pots with sharpenings in
and the shoes with no mud on them.

'Our school is a hardworking place,'
say the pencils writing, and a pile of paper,
and the pens marking.

'Our school is a colourful place,'
say the rainbows in the sky, the sun
and the moon, making night and day,
and the flowers making the whole world
brightly coloured.

'Our school is a well-mannered place,'
say the kids helping everyone.

Kellie Bettell (8)
St Helen's CE Primary School, Cliffe

LOUDLY

The horses kick at their door.
A mouse was squeaking in its hole.
A bird was flapping its wings.
A tractor came driving in.
A bee was buzzing in a tree.
A window was smashing.
A pig was snoring and -
loudest of all -
is a tiger roaring for its mum.

Leigh Ann Loveridge (8)
St Helen's CE Primary School, Cliffe

OUR SCHOOL

'Our school is a noisy place,'
say the stomping shoes,
slamming doors and rattling fence.

'Our school is a small place,'
say the chairs, toy cupboards and books.

'Our school is a tidy place,'
say the closed doors, clean floors
and chairs locked in.

'Our school is a hardworking place,'
say the worn out pencils, black rubbers and
aching wrists.

'Our school is a colourful place,'
say the shining displays, shining daisies
and the green grass.

Caroline Wollage (8)
St Helen's CE Primary School, Cliffe

OUR SCHOOL

'Our school is a tidy place,' say the clean tables and the tidy cupboards.
'Our school is a fair place,' say the fish and the flowers.
'Our school is a kind place,' say the books and the walls.
'Our school is the best place,' say the trays and the crayons.
'Our school is a learning place,' say the pencils and the rubbers.
'Our school is a posh place,' say the posh chairs and the posh tables.
'Our school is a fancy place,' say the dresses and trousers.

Mark Ebbs (8)
St Helen's CE Primary School, Cliffe

OUR SCHOOL

'Our school is a tidy place,'
say the clean floors,
pencils in pots and new shining books.

'Our school is not a lazy place,'
say the tucked-in chairs,
finished work and tidy displays.

'Our school is a posh place,'
say the teachers in suits,
the teachers in dresses
and the children in school uniforms.

'Our school is a big place,'
say the big halls
and the long corridors.

'Our school is a quiet place,'
say the closed mouths
and platform shoes

'But our school is the best,'
says me!

Lorna Towens (8)
St Helen's CE Primary School, Cliffe

OUR SCHOOL IS . . .

'Our school is tidy,' said the rubbish in the bins.
'Our school is big,' said the long fence.
'Our school is a colourful place,' said the dark blue paint.
'Our school is a clean place,' said the shiny floor.
'Our school is a working place,' said the pens writing.

Matthew Clough (9)
St Helen's CE Primary School, Cliffe

OUR SCHOOL

'Our school is not a quiet place,'
say the kids shouting,
the banging lunch boxes and the *bibbing* cars.

'Our school is a clean place,'
say the pots of varnish, the polished tables,
the sparkling floors.

'Our school is a colourful place,'
say the pretty flowers, the green trees,
and the singing daisies.

'Our school is not a lazy place,'
say the jumping kids, the hissing rulers
and the rattling pencils.

'Whatever happens to this place.
It will still be the *best!*'
Says me!

Nicola Wood (9)
St Helen's CE Primary School, Cliffe

ANIMAL MASQUERADE

Bet you'd never guess that a twig is an inchworm.

Bet you'd never guess that a load of weed is a crocodile.

Bet you'd never guess that grass is a grasshopper.

Natasha Rixson (9)
St Helen's CE Primary School, Cliffe

LISTEN

To the snow fall
on people's houses.
Listen to the
summer sunshine.
Listen.

Ray Woods (10)
St Helen's CE Primary School, Cliffe

AUTUMN NIGHT

Listen
to the owl screeching
as the leaves blow around houses.
Trees have begun to blow their treetops.
Listen.

Amy Slater (10)
St Helen's CE Primary School, Cliffe

NOVEMBER NIGHTS

November nights with a million flights of birds across the sky,
I can only just catch them in the corner of my eye.
How eagerly they fly when I look outside my window,
I think of tomorrow but then I think 'cold.'
And my toast would be covered with mould,
So now it's the sixth and seventh of November,
November the sixth and seventh of November.

Jacob Barnes (9)
St Peter's Methodist Primary School, Canterbury

MY FUTURE

Will there be trees
and will leaves still be on trees?

Will there be
people with eyeballs
popping out?

Will grannies be
grandads and grandads
be grannies?

Will aliens come
to invade Earth?

Will people have
1000 legs?

Daniel Scott
St Peter's Methodist Primary School, Canterbury

ICKIYOO THE INTERNATIONAL CAT

Ickiyoo the international cat,
Has jobs for this and jobs for that.
For instance, once he went on telly,
But lost his job, he had a smelly belly!

Hey wait, that was just the first time,
(I think this poem is starting to rhyme).
There was once when he went on the forecast
But all he could say was:
'Miaow, miaow, miaow!' very fast!

Joshua Gauton (8)
St Peter's Methodist Primary School, Canterbury

DOPPY THE DONKEY CAT

His ears are big
His nose is flat
He is the donkey cat.

Short legs
Loud laugh
He lives upon a farm.

His ears are big
His nose is flat
He is the donkey cat.

People think he's very weird
I just think he's cool
But most of all he's mine.

His ears are big
His nose is flat
He is the donkey cat.

Edward Noel (8)
St Peter's Methodist Primary School, Canterbury

TOPSY-TURVY LAND

Stop is go,
Sea turns to sand.
Everything is backwards
In Topsy-Turvy land.

Day is night,
Your feet are your hands.
Your room is downstairs
In Topsy-Turvy land.

Rachel Turner (8)
St Peter's Methodist Primary School, Canterbury

No!

No sun,
No moon,
No planets,
No sky,
No school,
No maths,
No art,
No English,
No plants,
No trees,
No creatures,
No warmth,
No cold,
No showers,
No sun.
No music,
No flute,
No tap,
No sound,
November.

Allanah Leonard-Booker (8)
St Peter's Methodist Primary School, Canterbury

THE WARM GLOW OF THE FIRE

I was walking outside in the freezing cold,
Looking into the bright and bold.
The smell of chicken in the air,
Even the fire made me look and stare!
The children jumping up and down
But I could only look and frown.

Rosie Pelham (8)
St Peter's Methodist Primary School, Canterbury

A COLD FREEZING NIGHT

It is a cold, freezing night,
First he sees a nice, warm light.
When out here it is cold and ice,
They are in the warm with no ice in there!

I live in the cold, icy street,
They live in a nice, hot house and eat meat.
It is warm, cosy, comfy chairs,
All I have to eat is pears.

They have hot, hot tea,
I drink water, water and water.
I am freezing,
They are warm.

The cat is sleeping,
Steam coming out of the kettle.

Welcoming candles for grandad,
A warm cup of tea when he comes
And a comfy chair for him.

Richard Puri (9)
St Peter's Methodist Primary School, Canterbury

MIKE THE MENACING CAT

Menacing here, menacing there
Mike the menacing cat is everywhere.
Up and down the stairs
Menacing like Dennis.
The menace is here and there
You just can't see him anywhere.

Tom Reece (7)
St Peter's Methodist Primary School, Canterbury

NOVEMBER

November.
Leaves on the
ground in November.
Frost on the
cars in November.

Fog on the
grass in November.
Bare trees
in November.

It's all
misty
in November.
Do you like November?

Devorah Shapiro (8)
St Peter's Methodist Primary School, Canterbury

MONDAY MORNINGS

Classrooms, cars and flowers
I see in school
All around me.
I see the lovely things they have in school,
Hopscotch,
Painted walls,
Decorated classrooms,
Sponge balls,
Tennis racquets,
All for me to see on a Monday.

Kieran Baldwin (9)
St Peter's Methodist Primary School, Canterbury

SPORTS TASTIC

Skateboarding down the street,
Concentrating to stay up straight,
Skateboarding tastic to every one I meet.

Swimming down the pool,
Getting rather tired,
Swimming tastic - isn't it cool.

Kicking the ball over the field,
Kicking up the grass,
I'm on my way to get the shield.
            Score tastic!

Dorothy Raphael (8)
St Peter's Methodist Primary School, Canterbury

FELIX THE FOOTBALLER CAT

Felix, felix the footballer cat,
He's a football fan,
Everyone's that!
At the moment he's playing for Brazil,
Now that's because everyone's ill!

Felix, felix the footballer cat,
Wait a minute what's that?
Oh look there's a rat!
Felix, felix there's no time for that!
Felix, felix the footballer cat.

Yasmin Harake (9)
St Peter's Methodist Primary School, Canterbury

EVERYTHING I ENJOY

Everything I enjoy
Wouldn't happen if I weren't a boy,
I love to go on country walks
And listen to quite grown-up talks.

I just love those castle walls
High above the inside halls.
I'd really like to have a dog
Who secretly lived inside a hollow log.

If I had a bicycle ride,
I'd love to go to a castle wide.

Jonathan Rogers (8)
St Peter's Methodist Primary School, Canterbury

OUTSIDE AT NIGHT

Christmas Eve in a cold winter tunnel
Walking through with no way of going
Begging for food and money
No name, no shoes, no place to go.

In the distance joyful people eating by a fire
Children in bed, snug with their ted.
Out of the tunnel
Knocking on doors, asking for a place for a night.

Luke Ryan (9)
St Peter's Methodist Primary School, Canterbury

DAYS IN NOVEMBER

I remember in November
The days I used to have
Slipping and sliding on the ice
Oh the days I used to have.

I remember in November
The days I used to have
The 5th of November was the best
The fireworks go bang!

Victoria Russ (9)
St Peter's Methodist Primary School, Canterbury

DENMARK THE DASHER CAT

Denmark Dasher is so fast,
Denmark Dasher is never last.
Denmark Dasher wins the race,
Denmark Dasher is the ace.
No other cats are like him,
Neither is his friend Tim.

Natalie Potts (9)
St Peter's Methodist Primary School, Canterbury

QUICKLY

Quickly I demolished that grumpy face,
Quickly I raced from that horrible face,
Quickly I left that grumpy face,
Quickly that face was a happy face.

Jordan Gosbee (9)
St Peter's Methodist Primary School, Canterbury

WILDLY

Wildly I jump out of bed,
Wildly I hit my head.
Wildly my cat will shout,
Wildly I let him out.

Wildly I get dressed,
Wildly I eat my breakfast (that's the best)!
Wildly I brush my hair,
Wildly my mum shouts 'Take some care!'

Alison Gauden (9)
St Peter's Methodist Primary School, Canterbury

SPIKE THE SPY CAT

Spike the spy cat is sneaking somewhere,
Don't go near him he'll give you a scare.
He is everywhere you go
But you really need to know,
Spike the spy cat is sneaking somewhere,
Don't go near him he'll give you a scare.

Ilyaz Hajat (8)
St Peter's Methodist Primary School, Canterbury

A COLD NIGHT

Snow is falling on my feet,
Snow is falling on my hands.
I'm standing here cold and white,
Waiting, waiting, waiting . . . to go outside.

Sam Swain (9)
St Peter's Methodist Primary School, Canterbury

CHEERFULLY

Cheerfully the old man mounts the stile,
Cheerfully the carthorse pulls his mile.
Cheerfully the tide creeps up the sand,
Cheerfully the shadows cross the land.

Cheerfully the hands move round the clock,
Cheerfully the dew dries on the dock.
Cheerfully I get fed,
Sadly I go to bed.

Francesca Barrett (9)
St Peter's Methodist Primary School, Canterbury

NOISILY

Noisily the children wake up,
Noisily the grown-ups drink from a cup.
Noisily the children get dressed,
Noisily they pretend to go on a quest.
Noisily they go to school,
They think their teachers are cruel.

Marilyn Haddock (9)
St Peter's Methodist Primary School, Canterbury

WHAT IS THE MOON?

The moon is a banana,
The moon is a white light,
The moon is a mirror
Shining at night.

Craig Bowler (8)
St Peter's Methodist Primary School, Canterbury

BUBBLES

Bubbles popping, bubbles bursting,
Bubbles floating away,
Bubbles popping every day,
I love bubbles.

Bubbles popping, bubbles bursting,
Bubbles, bubbles all through the day,
Bubbles slowly floating away,
I love bubbles.

Claire Scott (8)
St Peter's Methodist Primary School, Canterbury

THE ROARING SEA

I like the roaring sea,
        The shiny sand,
        The crumbling cliffs,
The soft sand goes everywhere when you hold it
The ocean blue sea will splash you.

I like the noisy seagulls in the sky,
        The bright sun,
        The blowing breeze,
The gloomy sky up high,
The sunset setting as we go.

I like the tones of the boats in the bay,
        The calm sea,
        The restful sea,
The sea around the boats,
The sweeping sea between the boats.

Kaley Wilder (11)
South Avenue Junior School

NIGHTMARE

One night I woke up screaming
I had been dreaming.
I shot up in despair when
I noticed I was covered in hair.
I ran down to the garden shed
and there I saw a floating head.
The floating head just disappeared.
How weird!
I went in and was ready to hide
when I spied a huge spider.
Out of its mouth flew a rat
with a wing of a bat.
I ran upstairs, climbed into bed
and said,
'I wish it would go away and
come back another day.'

Emma Persaud (10)
South Avenue Junior School

SOME CATS

Some cats live in houses,
Some cats live in flats,
Some cats are very large,
Some cats are very small,
Some cats are hunters,
Some cats are not,
Some cats are wild,
Some cats are tame,

But the cat I like best of all is my aunty's cat, Pat.

Kirsty Cunningham (11)
South Avenue Junior School

THE HAUNTED HOUSE

In the dark, dusty dungeon is a coffin
with cobwebs and creepy-crawlies.
Inside are some big silver chairs
and a murderous mummy.
Racing rats and barmy bats come out
And the only sound is a screaming spirit.

In the dark, gloomy attic is a painting
with its eyes popping out
staring at me as if I've done something wrong.
There's shaky shadows racing around all over the place
And the only sound is the creaking of the door.

In the dark, creepy ballroom
are chairs creeping around up and down.
There is a table dancing with the chairs.
Suddenly my feet start to move,
I'm dancing with the skeletons
And the only sound is the rattling
of the bones.

In the cold, dirty kitchen are
knives and forks flying around.
Food is flying everywhere, the knives
cut the bread in the air.
Suddenly everything falls to the ground 'bang'
And the only sound is the whistling of the wind.

Elizabeth Baker (10)
South Avenue Junior School

THE HAUNTED HOUSE

In the attic are
A box full of toys, torturing teddy bears
A painting with moving ears so it can hear you talking
And a moving chair going back and forth
And on the floor are cobwebs all over the place
And the only sounds are shaking skeletons.

In the tower there are:
Rotten rats
Trembly tarantulas
Slimy skeletons
Barmy bats
And the only sound is the slimy skeletons
coming up the stairs.

In the deep, dark dungeon is
A coffin with cobwebs and creepy-crawlies on it
Screaming skeletons hanging on the ceiling by a chair
shouting for help
And the only sounds are screaming spirits.

In the cellar are:
Gloomy ghosts
Smelly rats
Cobwebs and
Moths and mould,
And the only sound is the wine bottles
slamming together.

Abbi Little (11)
South Avenue Junior School

SUBMARINE

On the ground you are safe,
You are comfortable, you are great
But out at sea you will fear,
A dark predator at your boat's rear.

Beneath the waves it will stalk you,
It will hunt you, it will kill you.
You are at the mercy of the marines,
Coming up behind you in their submarines.

Towering high above your ship,
Powerless, you seem unable to stop it.
Guns are aiming at your boat,
You wonder, will we stay afloat?

You are horrified, you are terrified,
Its destructive power set on you.
The periscope, looking into your eyes,
So silent you can only hear the flies.

The marines start to board your boat,
You are taken prisoner.
Time is flying by too quick,
You really want to be seasick.

You wake up, it was all a dream,
But your room is not the same.
Nothing around you, not even a bell,
You are in a submarine cell.

James Cowden (10)
South Avenue Junior School

I Like The Seaside

I like the deep, dark, marine-blue sea,
I like the way the gentle, calm sea,
Turns into a rumbling, roaring ocean at night.
The way the waves swish to and fro then crash into the
cliffs and then die down.

        I like the sharp seashells.
        The way some feel as smooth as silk and some
        feel as rough as crumbly rocks,
        I like the beautiful and rusty colours of the shells.

I like the old, dark boats in the sea,
The smooth, new, fresh boats and the old, dark, rusty boats,
I like the way they set off into the gentle sea
and then disappear into the silent mist.

        I like the bumpy, soft sand,
        The way it feels and looks like camel humps.
        I like the way, the sand slips through my fingers
        when I pick it up,
        It is almost as though I'm holding shiny,
        little pieces of gold in my hands.

I like the seaside,
The silent sea at day,
The sharp shells on the beach,
The golden sand everywhere,
And the rusty, old boats in the sea,
The seaside is definitely a lovely place to be.

Rachel Cope (11)
South Avenue Junior School

THE HAUNTED HOUSE

Creepy cockroaches climbing cabinets,
With screaming shadows shaking in the candles,
And zany zombies hiding in the cellar,
And they're all coming to get me!

Terrifying tombs,
With broken bones inside,
And rapid rats running madly,
And they're all coming to get me!

Gooney goblins,
With slimy heads hanging from their mouths,
And mad mummies walking wildly,
And they're all coming to get me!

A cobweb-covered coffin,
With a very scary vampire inside,
And his teeth are as long as fingers,
And they're all coming to get me
And have me for tea!

Joe Hanson (11)
South Avenue Junior School

THE VOLCANO

The lava is as
hot as the sun.
The lava is as red
as blood. The lava splashes
like the sea in and out of rocks
raging through the street. The
blasting is like a bomb. The rumbling
shakes the world. The roaring is like an angry lion.

Harry Bushrod (10)
South Avenue Junior School

A LONELY ONE

A lonely leopard,
Prowls his domain,
Deep in a snowy tor,
Seeking prey for his den's supply of food,
He sees,
He smells,
A stoat in a large pine tree,
A lonely leopard,
Pounces!
A flash!
A bite!
A death-blow for a stoat.
Yet,
Another day
For a lonely leopard
Who prowls his domain.

Liam Marsh (10)
South Avenue Junior School

ANIMAL POEM

Today I saw a four-legged animal,
It had six tails and two fangs,
It had a gigantic beak and it had fur growing out of its ears,
Its wings were like a jumbo jet's, they were ginormous,
It had a lot of feathers on it,
It had little scales on its head,
And finally I saw its enormous talons like, a falcon's.
I don't think it was a normal animal,
It looked like a
mythological animal.

Anthony Seymour
South Avenue Junior School

THE MARINE-BLUE SEA

The marine-blue sea embracing and treasuring the secrets of the deep,
Mysteriously
The calm serene beach and the creatures so silent they seem asleep,
Magically,
The wet sand glistens like priceless gold,
Secretly.
Musical waves whisper their continuous song,
Calmly.

Seagulls soaring in the salty, atmospherical sky,
Ravenously.
The sea breeze whistles gently, it seems to die,
Gradually.
The lighthouse on top of the cliffs waiting for the night,
Patiently.

The yacht's mast, towers above the rippling surface of the water,
Motionlessly.
The sea waves lap against the harbour wall,
Swiftly.
Distant purple silhouettes of islands floating on the horizon,
Quietly.
Ship-like vessels cruise through the waves funnelling smoke,
Steadily.

Just thinking of the marine-blue sea swaying in my mind paints
a picture,
Beautifully.

Laura Palmer (10)
South Avenue Junior School

It's A Mysterious Cat

It treads silently across the garden
Creeping slowly in the shadows
Its eyes gleam and flash
It's a mysterious cat.

> Don't mess with this cat
> I've seen it pounce and kill a victim
> Its claws are razor-sharp
> It's a killer cat.

It's not like any other cat
Its teeth are sharp like knives
It's wild and wicked
It's a murderous cat.

> It stalks the garden all night long
> Its whiskers twitch like mad
> It sniffs the air with its button nose
> It's a curious cat.

You would look at this cat
And think it was sweet
But really it's a hunter
It's a ferocious cat.

Sarah Woolley (10)
South Avenue Junior School

Dolphins All Day

Dolphins swim and dolphins dive,
They need to survive by the ocean drive,
They swim all day while catching their prey,
And lie asleep for the newcoming day.

Graham Mark Wilson (10)
South Avenue Junior School

FORMULA ONE RACING DRIVER

F lying past the crowds
O ver the gravel trap
R iding at 200mph
M ulticoloured car
U pside-down and out of the race
L apping the slower cars
A t Suzaku, Japan

O ily track in front of me
N ew tyres are put on my car
E ngines roaring viciously

R acing round the track
A fter the leader
C hampion 3 years running
I n the Ferrari team
N eed more petrol
G oodyear tyres are put on as well

D riving madly down
R unning down the last bit
I 've won the race, champ 4 years running
V isor on my helmet gleaming
E mptying the car it
R ests till next year.

Antony Skillen (10)
South Avenue Junior School

THE OCEAN

I like the fishing boats in the harbour.
The smell of fresh fish,
The smell of damp seaweed,
The azure-coloured sea clashing against the white cliffs,
The bright-coloured crabs that get washed up at the sandy beach.

I like the sunny days at sandy beaches.
The lovely sea air,
The squawking seagulls,
The multicoloured starfish floating about in rock pools,
The graphite-coloured dolphins dancing in the ocean.

I like the chalky-white cliffs.
The crumbling rocks,
The diving seagulls,
The misty horizon disappearing in the distance,
The misty-white clouds towering over the cliffs.

I like the large slippery rocks.
The brown-coloured seaweed,
The chilling sea breeze,
The whale's blow-hole surfaces the sea,
The gleaming fish swim in schools.

Fraser Apps (10)
South Avenue Junior School

THE HAUNTED HOUSE

In the attic is:
        A red rat running races.
        A black bat fluttering upside-down.
        A smelly skeleton rotting away.
        A sprinting spider all around.
        A creepy coffin with a body inside.
        And the only sound I can hear is shaking souls.

In the attic is:
        A box of cranky claws.
        A mumbling mummy.
        Boxes of old torturing toys.
        A zooming zombie.
        A haunted holy ring.
        And the only smell I can smell is rotting eggs.

In the attic is:
        A ghostly goblin with bad manners.
        A dashing dragon chasing mice.
        A book of weird words.
        A slimy snake around my leg.
        A freaky man stomping around.
        And the only thing that I can see is a spirit.

In the attic is:
        A famous Frankenstein walking around.
        A piece of poisoned apple.
        A haunted book of spells.
        A cobweb with a gigantic spider.
        A wooden pencil writing invisible messages.
        And the only thing I can feel is a lamp with no bulb.

Emma Taylor (11)
South Avenue Junior School

THE HAUNTED HOUSE

Hello Mr And Mrs Frankenstien
And welcome!
Let me show you around.

First the great hall
Here you will find
Shaking chandeliers
A scary staircase,
The smell is wonderful,
A mixture of rotten rats, barmy bats and crazy cats
With the sound of the shackles down below.

We move onto the kitchen
You will find here,
Eerie earwigs
Trembling tarantulas,
A petrified poltergeist
And the smell of mouldy mildew
And the sound of the booming bells.

Now downstairs to the dungeon
You will find,
Shiny shackles,
Mumbling mummies
And creepy cobwebs
With the smell of rotting skeletons
And the sound of the screaming slaves of the dead.

So will you buy this wonderful house
With all its accessories?

Thomas Field (11)
South Avenue Junior School

THE SEA IS TRANQUIL IN THE BAY

The sea is tranquil in the bay,
It is perfect for bathing,
The crashing of the waves out at sea,
Makes you shiver in the night,
Lapping onto the cold cave floor,
Making your feet tingle.

A boat is motionless inside the harbour wall,
Others speed across the bay,
No mercy for the lonely rotting boats,
As they skulk washed-up on the shore,
The fearless boat tackles waves as high as itself,
Crashing against them with nothing to fear.

An island off a coastline,
Is appearing and disappearing,
You can see it has golden sand,
With shells that are large and bold,
Crabs have found homes in the smaller ones,
On the soft, silky sand.

The crumbling cliffs catch your eye,
With beauty just about to die,
The moss gives them an aged look,
Which makes you want to look,
This heritage is about to die,
It makes you sad and makes you cry.

James Field (11)
South Avenue Junior School

In The Dark Night There Was A . . .

In the dark night there was an explosion of colour,
Then an outburst of blue and pink.
In the dark night, there was a thrill and a dash
Then a dazzling *boom!*
In the dark night, there was a creation of colour
Then a gigantic, frightening scream.
A spectacular splutter of blue, green, yellow and red falling stars
which came pouring down.
In the dark night, there was an eruption and an outburst of blue
and purple.
In the dark night, there was a swirling and a spinning green and yellow
went going here and going there.
In the dark night, there was a diving and a dash and a bang
all in lime green!
In the dark night, there was a spring of gold then a
Crack and a screech of purply-pink.
In the dark night, there was a *spurt* of royal-blue.
In the dark night, there was a flickering green, a bursting
sparkling *whiz.*
In the dark night, there was an ear-bursting bang, then a diving scream.
In the dark night there was a quiet squeal to end it all.

Kayleigh Mitchell (11)
South Avenue Junior School

The Bottlenose Dolphin

Skimming, diving across the water gliding.
Aerobatics, somersaults, plunging deep and doing vaults.
Whistling, clicking, fins and tail flicking.
Caring, sharing, the bottle-nosed dolphin.

Rachel Vincent (9)
South Avenue Junior School

FIREWORK NIGHT

As we leave the car in the freezing night, people chatter,
At last the first screamer goes up,
I get out my money to get a burger,
The man behind the grill scrunches it into his pocket.

I walk to watch the *fizzling* fantasy whilst the ketchup
oozes from the side of the burger.
A huge *bang!*
As a screamer explodes in the sky.

I run to meet my parents by the bonfire,
I expect a wave of heat to hit me,
It doesn't happen,
The people's bodies lock the heat away from me,
I finally get through to find,
      It's gone!

I find my mum and dad,
'Let's go,' my dad says, sadly.
The gates slam after another *fun-fizzled* year.

Mathew Beech (11)
South Avenue Junior School

AT THE COAST

The rough sea crashing ferociously against the cliff,
The smooth sand blows slowly across the beach,
Some scaly fish swim calmly in the sea,
Vicious sharks drift, hungry for their prey,
The orange sunset glistens in the red sky,
The lighthouse blinks brightly on top of the cliff,
The twinkling stars gleam in the night sky.

Michael Morris (11)
South Avenue Junior School

FIREWORKS WHIZZING

F ireworks whizzing up and down the garden.
I nteresting food for all the family.
R ockets here, rockets there, all the rockets are everywhere.
E njoying bombs, bangers and money in pockets.
W orking men missing out.
O ver the moon, goes the rockets.
R oman candles in the gardens.
K eeping memories of Guy Fawkes.
S earching for screamers as the Catherine wheel spins.

W atch out for the sparklers from the fireworks or they'll go in
   your eyes.
H ustling and bustling as the crowd try to see the fireworks.
I s it warm or is it me?
Z ooming, zang, zong, goes the fireworks in different directions.
Z oooommmm go the pets in the house as the screamers shriek.
I n go the people for a brilliant Thursday dinner.
N obody moves as the last fireworks go off into the dark night.
G ee, I wonder whether it would be as good as this year again?
   But surely no one could better our fireworks display.

Rebecca Mayne (11)
South Avenue Junior School

THE CAT AND PAT

There once was a cat,
Who lived in a hat.
Along came Pat (his friend).
The cat climbed out of the hat,
The cat and Pat sat on the mat.
Then they gave each other a pat on the back.

Marcus Childs (10)
South Avenue Junior School

As I Walk Along The Sand

As I walk along the sand
I see,
Sweet shaking shells that look like shaking pocket pets.
I see,
A sleeping seagull that looks like a sleeping baby.
I see,
Slimy, smelly seaweed that looks like a shaky hand.
I see,
Sharp shingle that looks like sharks' teeth.

As I walk along the sand
I see,
Colourful cuttlefish that look like a cunning pearl.
I see,
Calm clouds that look like clumps of cotton wool.
I see,
Colossal cliffs that look like camouflaged sand dunes.
I see,
Cute canoes that look like containers of paint.

Samantha Spokes (11)
South Avenue Junior School

Fireworks

Fireworks spinning in the sky.
Fireworks exploding in the sky.
Fireworks spitting a shower of colours in the sky.
Fireworks screaming in the sky.
Fireworks banging in the sky.
Fireworks standing there . . .
I wonder why?

Adam Wilder (11)
South Avenue Junior School

THE HAUNTED HOUSE

In the creepy attic are
Horrified horrors spooking me out.
A doll with her hair raising.
A painting with moving eyes and closing them at night.
A freaky Frankenstein teddy.

In the creepy attic is
A box of old toys.
Clothes everywhere but it was never like that on Monday.
A box that looked like a coffin with all creepy crawlies on it,
I opened it, it was a mummy.

In the creepy attic is
A box of witch clothes
I thought, am I dreaming?
'No you are not' said a voice.
I run down the stairs as fast as my legs would carry me
And never went up there again.

Sarah Pearce (11)
South Avenue Junior School

THE HAUNTED HOUSE

Bang!
Goes the door, another ghost haunting the house.
The roof is rattling and clattering as someone walks across it.
My expensive wine is being drunk by a ghost,
Another one hundred pounds down the drain.
My disappearing Dalmatian dog.
Husky howling from behind the bookcase.
I can hear the breaking of the stained glass windows.
Everyone dreads going near here.

Louise Marie Duke (11)
South Avenue Junior School

THE FIREWORK DISPLAY

Bang!
The first firework goes off, it's colourful
Then it's gone and the black night looks plain
Firing into the sky, then appears another lot of colours
Everybody is dazzled by the fireworks
As I stand back, up go the fiery fountains.

The colours die down from the sky
Shooting one by one, they all whizz up
The child next door plays with a sparkler
They let off the Catherine wheels, that's what I like best
Blue, yellow, red and green lies in the sky.

They open another box
And up goes another rocket
It's sizzling scarlet
It's the end of the firework display
And I'm exhausted
I wonder if we'll come next year, I do hope so.

Marcus Kelly (11)
South Avenue Junior School

LIMERICKS

There was an old man called Bill
Who had a great big pill
He was very hot
He came out in spots
The next day he was very ill.

Amelia Godley (10)
South Avenue Junior School

THE HAUNTED HOUSE

I open the front door, step in and
Bang!
The door closes.
The ground thumping like a heart and then the
Floorboards lift.
As I go up the decaying stairs, they start to make
An eerie sound.
I go in the bedroom, no sound just a cold breeze up my back.
I go out on the balcony, creepy footsteps come my way.
Slam! I shut the balcony doors.
I go up the winding stairs to the attic, I hear ghostly sounds.
In the dark corners of the room I hear a commotion.
Further up the winding stairs, I come to the bell tower.
I see flying bats and then I hear a small whisper.
I rush downstairs and I shut the cellar door.
Then the wine bottles start to float around and I hear rats and mice.
I run out the house, down the hill, down my street
And *bang!* I shut the door.

Terry Clarke (10)
South Avenue Junior School

CATS

I see his eyes glowing in the dark.
They are red with a black line in the middle.
His eyes shut a little bit.
His sharp claws dig in my arms.
His tail is smooth and he can move it in funny ways.

Ben Deragon (10)
South Avenue Junior School

THE MIDNIGHT HUNT

Late at night a tiger creeps out of sight.
The moon shines on him like a spotlight,
Showing the face of a killer at night.
He creeps around not making a sound,
Apart from those who are underground.
He crosses the streams, rivers and more,
Till he comes to a place famous to all.
A hunting place, with lots of gazelles,
With dark brown horns and fluffy white tails.
He's chosen his animal, he's chosen his spot.
He's running so fast he can't even stop!
His claws are digging into the ground,
He's leaping forwards onto the gazelle.
His bone-crunching teeth as sharp as knives,
Are digging quite deep, he's sure got his prize.
The gazelle's on the floor, he's pulling it away,
He's taking it back for his cubs today.

Anita Hills (10)
South Avenue Junior School

THE FIREWORKS

F is for fantastic.
I   is for incredible.
R is for releasing.
E is for energy.
W is for wonderful.
O is for orange.
R is for rain.
K is for kind.
S is for sun.

Robert Hoxey (11)
South Avenue Junior School

MIDNIGHT SNACK

Down the stairs,
Hear those shoes,
Try to think what to choose,
Fizzy drink,
Apple juice,
What about that big, thick mousse?

Up the stairs,
Into bed,
Better cuddle big, bad, ted.
Really scruffy,
A terrible smell,
I love him anyway as you can tell.

Michael Baxendale (8)
South Avenue Junior School

THE HAUNTED HOUSE

Crash goes the teapot as it rolls down the stairs.
Bats flying round the second floor and up the creaky stairs.
In the bell tower, the bell is ringing,
It sounds like an old rusty bit of tin.
Slam! The front door is shut.
A cold shiver goes up my spine.
I look in the mirror, I see the ghost
But he has no twinkle in his eyes.
It's 12 o'clock the witch dropped by her broomstick.
I chopped the broomstick into little bits.
The witch chopped me and that is it.
Now I'm the ghost of the bell tower.

Katie Bosley (11)
South Avenue Junior School

THE SEASIDE

I like the swaying, sparkling sea,
  The calm sea
  The tranquil sea
The sea smelling of seaweed and salt

I like the golden seagulls
  Gliding swiftly
  Eating hungrily
The seagulls dive underwater
Gliding here and gliding there

I like the soft sandy seaweed
  Warm and dusty
  Seaweed wet
Soggy seashells are on my feet
Sticky seaweed meets my feet.

Kimberley Murphy (10)
South Avenue Junior School

THE HAUNTED HOUSE

I was walking towards a haunted house,
On the way I saw a spooky mouse.
I sat on the porch, the door opened by itself,
As I went in, there was a *crash* and a *bang,*
I went in the lounge, I dashed with fright to see Adolf Hitler,
Into the kitchen with terror,
I saw Princess Diana baking,
I dashed to the cellar to see a rat with towering teeth,
I dashed to the bell tower to see *skeletons,*
So I raced to the bedroom only to see *ghosts,*
So in a flash I ran to the door and sped home.

Andrew Steven Wright (10)
South Avenue Junior School

THE SEASIDE

I like the bright blue boats out at sea,
The smell of seaweed in the sea,
The bright yellow light from the sea's sun,
And the beam of heat on the sea's beach.

I like the hot golden yellow sand on the beach,
Which always warms my hands and feet,
When I walk along the sea's beach,
I always look out at the sea.

I like the smell of hot dogs on the beach,
I eat them when walking along the sea,
Tomato ketchup falls all over my T-shirt,
I always give lots of bread to the birds.

Timothy Reynolds (10)
South Avenue Junior School

A VAN

As sharp as a dragon digging his claws into the tarmac road softly.
As shiny as a bar of gold floating softly.
As dazzling as a dolphin jumping softly.
As fast or slow as a tiger hunting softly.
As wonderful as a diamond spreading light softly.
As red as blood flowing softly through our veins.
As heavy as a 1000,000 pound weight rolling softly.
As quiet or loud as a lion creeping or growling softly.
As long as a bus driving softly.

Anthony Kay (9)
South Avenue Junior School

CATS

Some cats are crazy,
Some are just lazy.
Some cats might be bad,
Some might be sad.

Some cats are nice,
But not when they see mice.
Their eyes are very round,
Some never hear a sound.

My cat's the best,
I said to the rest.
He has pointed claws,
On his little paws.

Gemma Glover (10)
South Avenue Junior School

THE PANTHER

As the panther pounds from tree to tree,
Searching for his prey.
He looks, he sees, he jumps.
Fiercely he tears apart another victim.
Yet he has taken another life,
From the animal kingdom,
And will take again
But now he sleeps as sound as a bird.
Until morning comes again.

James Stuart (11)
South Avenue Junior School

THE 40 GHOSTS

One ghost is in the kitchen,
And one ghost is going to the bell tower,
And four ghosts are going to bed,
And two ghosts are going to scare the bats at 12 o'clock,
And one is at the door,
And six are breaking glass with stones,
And ten are going to the toilet,
And five are going to make dinner for their boss,
And ten are tidying the hallway,
And all 40 ghosts are lining up smartly dressed,
40 - that's a lot!
I wish I was not in that house.

Martyn James Jarrett (10)
South Avenue Junior School

FIREWORKS

Fireworks are fun, watch them shoot up to the sky.
When they reach the sky, colours explode.
Catherine wheels whizzing round making a *zzzz* noise.
Watch the Roman candles shooting out bright stars.
The sound of bombs whooshing off into the sky.
Sparklers lighting different patterns.
What a nice sight as traffic lights turn different colours,
First red, then yellow and green.

Oh no! The night has disappeared into silence.

Mikaela Jade Simmers (10)
South Avenue Junior School

Noisy Fireworks

Bang, pop, boom go the fireworks up into the sky.
The Catherine wheel crashing with a scream.
Everyone's faces light up where the fireworks crash and bang.

All of the fireworks start to die down.
They all disappear in the sky.
They make lots of noise.
Bright colourful fireworks red, blue and pink.
All zooming through the sky.

Everyone's going home now the fireworks have died down.
Now it's quiet, there's not a sound.

Joanna Oakley (11)
South Avenue Junior School

Purple

Dotted purple plums on a plum tree.
The purple bruise when you hit a stone in the sea.
Purply blossom in the beginning spring.
The juicy plum which gives a ting on your tongue.
Blueberry ice-cream with blueberry bite.
The sweet smell of spring scenting the air.
The lavender scattered, laying on the ground.
The scent of blossom bobbing on the breeze.
The dark purple sky on a stormy night
And the cold sensation of a purple room.

Melanie Laver (11)
South Avenue Junior School

THE LIGHTHOUSE

The towering lighthouse stands on top of the cliff
watching over the sea.
Its light rules the waves,
guiding the fishing boats to harbour.
The lighthouse keeper, old and grey.
The last in all the land
for the lighthouse will be automated.
The keeper to be relieved from the lighthouse on the cliff.
Which stands lonely in the wind.

Ben Conway (11)
South Avenue Junior School

THE DAY AT THE BEACH

The little crab snapping quickly,
At the cold stone rolling slowly,
Onto the soft sunset setting quietly,
With the tall ship rushing rapidly,
Disturbing the shiny sand, floating happily.

Jonathan Ward (10)
South Avenue Junior School

SUMMER

Summer.
Hot summer,
Sweating all over,
Feeling really thirsty and tired.
Summer.

Charlene Lucy Kay (10)
South Avenue Junior School

FIREWORKS

Fresh fireworks in the sky,
I really love fireworks,
Ready, steady, go.
Enormous colourful fireworks
Whizzing up, *bang!*
Oh wow! That was red, green, blue and yellow.
Red was that rocket,
'K'! Oh, the shape of 'K'.
Sorry, it's finished.

Jordon Pritchett (10)
South Avenue Junior School

WEATHER

Wind,
Wind, bristles through, brushes hair,
It runs through grass,
And kicks some glass,
It's all so, so fast.

Rain,
Rain, cries as it hits the floor,
It falls one thousand feet,
Then dies.
Then watches some more and pounces on you.

Sun,
Sun, glows as it's watching,
Thinking,
Waiting to throw,
To throw its glow.

Jonathon Stewart (10)
Thames View Junior School

SEASONS

The flowers grow, the wind dies down,
The snow melts like a pool of ice, the days get longer,
The sun shines bright, newborn life is born nearly every hour,
No brown leaves show, no snowmen about,
All's peace and quiet while the sun's about.

Now summer's here, the days get hot,
The newborn life is growing up, no pools of water from the snow,
As evening comes every day, the mountains of Switzerland look ablaze,
No brown leaves left, just green and white
For this is the season for fun, all right?

It's getting chilly for autumn's here, I need to *bbbrrr!* It's very chilly,
The leaves have turned brown and have fallen down,
The growing-up newborns are getting older,
The winds get stronger, the leaves get browner but
The last season's near so this poem will soon have to end.

Tut, tut, tut, the snowmen are back,
There's nothing to do except go and build a snowman yourself,
For Christmas is near, I must go now,
I have to get ready or I'll miss out.

Lauren Coombes (10)
Thames View Junior School

FIREWORKS

A flash in the dark that lights up the sky,
Cascading down to the burning Guy,
For hundreds of years on November 5th,
We remember the plot that gave us this gift,
Of fireworks, bonfires, sparklers and Guys.
That together this night light up the skies!

Alex Allen (9)
Thames View Junior School

MRS ANDY

Mrs Andy
Just loved candy,
She ate it every day,
She ate it until it was time to play.

'I love candy' she would boast,
It was what she liked the most,
'Sticky, sticky,' Mrs Andy said,
As she munched it in her bed.

But one day she had her fill,
She was very ill,
Poor old Mrs Andy,
She just had to give up candy.

Hayley Chapman (7)
Thames View Junior School

THE CANDLESTICK

A candle standing there alone.
It's shivering,
A black, red flame.
The candle
Melting away,
Getting smaller
And smaller.
The flame is
Burning out.

Carl Temple (10)
Thames View Junior School

A FISH CALLED CROWN

As
he swims
around and around
I wonder why I called him
Crown. It came across me once
before, I just don't know, I'm a bore.
As my fish swims around and around, I wonder
why I called him Crown. Why not Percy, Poodle or Pim,
Bubbles or Horris or Pooch or Jim?
In his bowl on the window sill,
he swims about and flicks
his gills. Then on his
bowl the sun shines
down and makes
him shine like
a king's
crown.

Charlotte Knight (10)
Thames View Junior School

MY BIG SISTER

My sister is a terror,
But Mum loves her more
than ever!
She thinks she is so
clever!
Compared to me *never!*
And that's my big
sister.

Aneesha Tiwari (7)
Thames View Junior School

When I Was A . . .

When I was a baby, I loved to play with toys,
I cuddled my mum really tight,
And always said 'goodnight'.

When I was a toddler, I could talk,
And walk too,
The best thing I could do was say 'moo'.

When I was a child, I went to school,
I could swim, turn off the light,
I could fly a kite.

Samuel Jordan (8)
Thames View Junior School

Hurricane

The hurricane ran swiftly through the sky,
Consuming everything that passed nearby.
It captured all things in its windy cell.
How much can it grasp?
I can't tell.
As it laughs madly and flies out of sight,
You can see the horror it left that night.

Hannah Baker (10)
Thames View Junior School

The Candle

The candle is sad and alone,
Can't talk to anyone,
Dancing slowly it's very sad,
Melting quickly because it's hot,
It's embarrassed to show what it's really like.

It's cosy as its flame keeps burning hot, hot, hot,
Shimmering from side to side,
It's not very happy as it's waving around,
It blows out and dies,
Goodnight.

Faye Andrew (10)
Thames View Junior School

LOTS OF CHILDREN BOASTING

Ha you! I know someone who carries fifty-one backpacks to school.
Yes, but er! I know someone with sixty-inch binoculars.
So what! I know someone who has one thousand clocks in his bedroom.
Oo really good! I know a girl in my old school who spits milk out of
                                                    her nose.
Um! I've got a mate who jumped off the Empire State Building and
                                        bounced back up to the sky.
But I'm better than all those people put together.
I've got hypnotic powers see . . . ! I made you say all that rubbish!

Paul More & Aaron Bass (9)
Thames View Junior School

MY POEM OF CANDLES

When I light my candle I feel excited,
The red candle with orange fiery flames,
The fragrance makes me think of wafty kindness,
The light, bright, hot wax is smoky,
I say to myself it's slimy,
Then all of a sudden, whoosh it's blown out and darkness appears,
There is silence,
It's all ready for tomorrow.

Roxanne Hemans-Davis (9)
Thames View Junior School

THE PEACEFUL CANDLE

As it slowly moves up and down,
I wonder what it may be thinking.
Is it floating in the air, or relaxing peacefully?
My candle looks trapped in a cage,
by wicked evil witches.
Is it trying to get away?
Is it trying to stay alive?
Is my candle saying 'Don't blow me out,
don't blow me out'?
Does it hurt to be on fire?
As the wax melts, I still think it's saying . . .
'Don't blow me out, let me live this peaceful life,
but please don't blow me out.'
The shining gold light of peace,
is swaying to and fro.
As it flickers up and down,
the bumpy trickles slide down the wax.
The warm colours amuse the children's anxious faces,
as it melts down and down.
Its two-coloured head wobbles,
side to side, up and down, left and right.
From the beginning of its life, to the end of its life,
may he have a peaceful life.
Is it still saying . . .
'Don't blow me out'?

Megan Wright (10)
Thames View Junior School

ENVIRONMENT

Look in the sky, what do you see?
I see a bird speaking to me.
Look what we're doing to the air
We are polluting the air and the world's children care.

Look at a forest getting cut down
Branches getting ripped off, I feel the pain.
Look what we're doing to the forests
Imagine you were the tree.

Clark Taylor (9)
Thames View Junior School

GROWING UP

When I was one,
I sucked my tiny thumb
And I was so dumb.
When I was two,
I licked my shoe
And got dirt on my tongue too.
When I was three,
I bumped into a big tree
And hurt my knee.
When I was four,
I went on a long tour
And lots more.
When I was five,
I was very much alive
And saw someone dive.
When I was six,
I tried a Twix
And ate a cake mix.
When I was seven,
I tried to see heaven
And went to Devon.
Now I am eight,
I have a good mate
And always shut the gate.

Hannah Ayres (8)
Thames View Junior School

NOCTURNAL ANIMALS

At night,
When I fall asleep,
I hear noises,
Not like distant music or traffic
But like animals.

Then I wonder,
What kind of animals come out at night?
Then I think about,
What animal could it be tonight?

Could it be . . .
A hedgehog with a snuffly sound?
Or maybe a fox drifting down the road?
Or could it be a wolf howling
At the moon
Waiting for a treat . . .
Perhaps a human?

There it was,
That sound again,
That monstery sound.
Oh I wish it would go away.
No, I wish dawn would come
And sweep all the demons elsewhere.

Katy Everett (10)
Thames View Junior School

TWINKLE CANDLE

The twinkle candle glows in the dark,
The twinkle candle is burning and blowing,
The twinkle candle has melting wax,
The twinkle candle is red,
How peaceful.

The twinkle candle is lovely and cosy,
The twinkle candle has a quiet flame,
The twinkle candle is glimmering,
The twinkle candle is sad and lonely,
Oh, now it burns out. Goodbye.

Carla Stepney (10)
Thames View Junior School

WRITING THANK YOUS

Dear Nan
Thank you for my bobbly hat,
and my Cindy,
I can't wait for winter!
Thanks!

Dear Aunt
Thank you for my pink pyjamas,
I'm sure I'll be snug and warm,
oh and those pink slippers!
Thanks.

Dear Uncle
Thank you for my purple spotted dress,
I'm sure I'll wear it for parties,
and that purple spotted ribbon!
Thanks!

Dear Mum and Dad
Thank you for that television, it's really great,
I'll be really warm in bed watching,
Friends of course!
Thanks very much!

Stephanie Cordes (9)
Thames View Junior School

FLICKERING ME

Here I am freezing cold and talking to my brothers,
Then all of a sudden I get brought out,
'Yes!' I scream,
Hearing that noise I like,
There it is gleaming like me when I'm alight,
'Yes!' I'm alight
I look around,
People are staring at me,
I look at them back,
I start to sweat and cry for joy,
But I know my time will soon be over,
People are just sitting there,
Staring at me,
I don't know why,
And then a tall lady bends over talking,
All of a sudden a gentle blow,
I try to move but then I say my prayers,
And then I go out,
My body tries to glimmer,
But up I go and away I go.

Robert Davies (9)
Thames View Junior School

SPARKLERS

Sparklers are very bright, they flicker and show up against
the dark night.
They shine like stars in the dark sky.
Always wear your gloves as they jump up the stick,
Oh no the sparkler is fading away and now it has gone out.
It is time for us to go home.

Rebecca Stone (9)
Thames View Junior School

ANTS

Ants, ants in your pants
sprinting down the road.
Some of them flying, some of them running
after the little boy Ronny.

Ants, ants in your pants
sprinting on the beach,
some of them surfing, some of them swimming
and then they got eaten by a shark.

Ants, ants in your pants
driving a sports car.
One of them pulls the clutch and one of them pushes the brake
and then they both smashed out of the window.

Ants, ants in your pants,
walking down the street
one of them runs forward, one of them runs backwards
and then the little boy Ronny stamps on them both.

Wesley Larkin (10)
Thames View Junior School

THE CANDLE GLOWS

One stormy night in a big castle
there was a big candle
glowing in the dark room.
There was a ghost
working by the candle.
The ghost said
'I've finished my candle poem at last.'
Then he had a party.

Michael Halpin (10)
Thames View Junior School

LITTLE GIRL

When I was a little girl
I used to drink all day long.
When I became one
I used to stumble on my fat little feet
Round and round and round.
I used to drink ink.

When I was a little girl
I sat on my potty
Like a big girl.
Then I did something wrong and I got told off.
My friend Lotty could nearly drive
And she was only five.

When I was a little girl
I got christened and I did a poo in the church.
The vicar went 'Whoa! That's a big one!'
Then I learnt to go 'hoo'!

Megan Kelly (9)
Thames View Junior School

WHEN I WAS FIVE

When I was five I went to school
but I didn't like it because the
teacher was cruel.

We all got told off and weren't
very happy
because the teacher was snappy.

At twelve o'clock it was time
to play and I couldn't wait
for the end of the day.

It was time to go home and
have some fun
so I got out of the door and
started to run.

Reece Nicholson (8)
Thames View Junior School

THE CANDLE

Leaving the gloomy, dark world behind him,
The red candle is slowly lit.
It flickers madly and shimmers very brightly
And lets out more fierce fires every now and then.
It proudly stands there growing,
Bigger and bigger.
It can see smiling faces staring at it,
He must have drawn their attention.
Then a scary face
Comes slowly down on him,
He's going to die, leave
Back to the cold days,
Back to a hard red statue,
Back to the dark cupboard,
He will leave the world behind him
And wait for that shaking noise
To come once more.
All he is now is a puff of smoke
Floating up to heaven.

Jenna Hearnden (10)
Thames View Junior School

WINDY

The wind was howling,
Sweeping up the leaves
Departed from their trees.

The wind roared,
And uprooted trees,
It ripped off houses' roofs
As if it had two arms.

It spat out cars, as if it had a mouth,
Hurling them into orbit.
It smashed glass windows
With a mighty, mighty blow.

It was as if it liked,
Making devastation.

Philip Hall (11)
Thames View Junior School

NIGHT

I can't sleep.
There's so many sounds.
There's distant cars.
The glistening stars.
There's flapping bats,
And wailing cats.
Shining moon in the sky.
Shadows of the trees.
I'm saying,
Be quiet please!

George Broom (11)
Thames View Junior School

THE DARKNESS OF THE NIGHT

At night I hear the wailing of the owl,
So delicate and sweet.
Then I hear the grasshopper go cheep, cheep,
I hear the foxes rustling in the bushes,
They give a ferocious shout.
I jump up in bed,
I hear the hedgehogs in the rubbish,
I quickly get up and run downstairs to stop them,
But they're gone.
I hear the traffic in the distance,
It is so peaceful in the dark night sky.
I saw the moon gleaming down at me,
So bright and shiny.
It is the best part of the day.

Steven Smith (11)
Thames View Junior School

THE BIRD AND THE ZEBRA

There was once a bird and a zebra,
Called Edder and Debra,
They went to Greece,
In a very greasy boat,
They were both sick,
They ended up in Wicks with the hics,
That's why the zebra is black and white.
That's why the duck went mad.
They did,
They did.
That's why the zebra turned pink and yellow.

Jennie Coles (9)
Thames View Junior School

I'M SORRY MISS

Miss, I forgot my homework
Stop making excuses up Bill
I'm not, honestly I'm not
Where is it then?
Um um
See you don't know!
My brother has torn it up
Bill are you lying?
No Miss, I'm not
Then you shouldn't leave it around
I didn't, he stood on a stool
You should have been watching him
I was but I looked around and he must have got it
Are you sure you didn't leave it at home?
Yes, I'm sure Miss. Ah, I remember now Miss
Where is it Bill?
I left it at my auntie's Miss, I think the dog ate it
What happened to the dog?
It died Miss
What did it die of?
Mepothonea Miss
What's that?
It's a terrible disease Miss, loads of dogs get it
Are you trying to change the subject Bill?
I am not, honestly I'm not
Oh here we go Miss.

Hannah Brooking (9)
Thames View Junior School

I'm Lit Again

The creaky cupboard slowly opens,
A gigantic hand comes in and touches me gently,
It takes me in a brightly coloured room,
All the shining lights are on
Apart from lonely old me,
Suddenly I hear the rattly noise I heard before,
I knew it,
It came back to make me happy,
Then the humans' hand swiftly strikes the match,
And I'm proud all shimmering like before,
Flickering brightly as my flames get bigger,
I'm nearly crying,
I feel so lucky,
I start dripping sweat,
It's so blistering and hot in here,
Or is it me,
I admire myself proudly,
It's like I'm in the hottest party ever,
I still flicker as my flames get bigger,
Then the gigantic face gets closer and closer,
I'm dreading this to happen again,
The big face blew me,
My spirits floated away in peace,
I hope I see the light of night-time again.

Jade Bentley (9)
Thames View Junior School

THE WILD WHISPERING WIND

The wild, whispering wind,
blows down tall trees.
It sweeps up colourful leaves
and causes rough seas!
The wild, whispering wind,
is very, very cold.
It bites at your skin,
so horrible to behold!
The wild whispering wind,
is so very, very strong,
It makes big bushes rustle,
tougher than King Kong!
The wild, whispering wind,
is faster than a bullet,
faster than a speeding cheetah,
nothing can stop it!

Jonathan Costello (11)
Thames View Junior School

NIGHT

Night is coming,
Time to go to bed.
Peace is coming,
Time to dream.
I can hear noises.
Time to relax.
All is dark.
I can see the moonlight,
Going across the river.
Now it's time to sleep.

Christopher McGarry (11)
Thames View Junior School

WHEN I WAS YOUNG

When I was small I was the size of a ball
I looked at the hall and said 'It's so tall!'

When I was named, my sister was playing games
Then she aimed and missed again!

When I was four, I could open a door
But then I fell on the floor and my bottom was sore.

When I was six, I played some tricks
And then I flicked a load of sticks.

Now I am eight, I am more awake
And life is like a piece of cake.

James Baker (9)
Thames View Junior School

WHEN I WAS YOUNG

When I was young I sucked my thumb
I didn't hurt my gums.
When I was two I fell down the loo
I also got hit by a pool cue.
When I was three my sister slapped me
So I wished I was twenty.
When I was four I put my fist through the door.
When I was five I learned to dive.
When I became six I was very sick.
When I was seven I learnt the word 'heaven'.
Now I am eight I wish to be nine
And that would make me feel just fine.

Carl Hearnden (8)
Thames View Junior School

THE HEDGEHOG AND THE PIG

The hedgehog and the pig went to Mars
In a super shiny rocket,
They took some soup and some Hula Hoops
Which sat in the pig's coat pocket.
After 5 minutes they had eaten the lot
And they got so fat,
The hedgehog sat down and broke the chair
So that was the end of that.
The hedgehog sang a lullaby
To the pig who was falling asleep,
But before the pig could drop off
The hedgehog fell asleep!
The pig was suddenly wide awake
And the hedgehog began to snore,
The pig sat down and then he said
'Oh this is such a bore!'
Then they reached Mars,
The hedgehog woke up
And the pig then shouted 'Hooray!'
They got off the rocket and the pig said,
'I could stay here all day.'
The hedgehog looked down to the Earth below and said
'Oh wow, it's round!'
Then they gasped and then they said,
'We are not on the ground!'
Indeed they were right,
They were still in the air
But there was nothing they could do,
        And they are still up there!

Faye Chapman (10)
Thames View Junior School

The Resplendent Flame

Waiting in the bleak cupboard,
Wanting to see light,
Wanting to come alive,
Wait, what's that rustle?
What's that creak?
Daylight!
Hey! Where are you taking me?
Please, I must know!
Hang on a minute,
I recognise that shape,
But I can't remember where from.
At last,
At last,
The moment I've been waiting for!
Yes, I'm lit!
Though I'm silent, that doesn't matter,
I don't want to be massive and destructive.
I'm just swaying, silently in the wind.
My flame is lighting up the night's sky,
Bringing all of the impatient stars to life,
Like a twinkle in your eye.
I'm flickering,
I'm quivering,
A spark has gone up,
So dazzling,
No! Please!
I'm going, going, going . . .
He's gone, going up to heaven.

Jade Hinksman (9)
Thames View Junior School

MY OLD MEMORIES

When I was tiny and just a baby,
I got all the attention and was popular.
Now I am older and don't get so much.
I wish I was small like before.
When I was small I was cherished.
Now that I'm older and better and intelligent
I think back to the past and say to myself
'Now that I'm older it's better.'
But then I think, 'I bet it will be better when I'm eighteen.'
So looking back, I got the attention
And looking forward I can make my decisions.
If I could time travel, I question where I would go -
The future or the past? That's confusing.
'I know, I'll go to the past.
No, I'll go to the future.
Oh no! Now I'm as confused as ever.
Well, I think I'd go the past, then I could plan for the future.'

Michael Baker (8)
Thames View Junior School

THE CANDLE

The candle flickering, flaming, dancing
Glowing, glowing, stretching
It's so sad and quiet
Although it's on a diet
He's quivering on his thighs
Embarrassed by the eyes
He's fading away
He will be back another day.

Aaron Mason (9)
Thames View Junior School

CANDLE

In a dark corner,
In a silent room,
A candle glows
In the gloom.
A quivering light,
What some sight.

The green wax is melting and rippling so,
The flame shimmering all alone,
Really dry down to the bone.

A breeze blows,
The candle goes out,
A smoky smell
And the light fell.

Maximillian Ferris (10)
Thames View Junior School

LONELY CANDLE

Glowing in a room of sadness,
Flickering all on its own.
The candle burning all alone,
The scented smell from wet, red wax.
A shadowy figure standing proudly,
The flame rising very tall.
It's dancing in a warm room,
The wind blows a spark.
A twinkle looks upon the darkness,
My candle is dying very slowly.

Matthew Peter Baker (10)
Thames View Junior School

SOMETHING WATCHING ME

As I walked down the garden in the dark,
I could hear the singing of a lark,
As I scratched my head,
I wished I was in bed,
As I listened I heard the buzz of a bee,
But all the time something was watching me.

I could not see them just then,
It could have been a hen,
As I turned around,
I could not hear a sound,
But as I walked up to the house,
I could hear a tiny mouse,
It could have been a he or a she,
But something was still watching me.

Rhys Barnish (11)
Thames View Junior School

THE DYING CANDLE

The candle is a tall, straight
Sad looking guy.
It is flaming and bright,
Bent over one way.
When it is dancing
It flickers and reflects
On the lovely smelly candle
But when you go to blow it out,
It sadly waves
  Goodbye.

Steven Clare (9)
Thames View Junior School

THE LONELY CANDLE

As the lonely candle starts to flicker continuously
It gets lighter and lighter.
Tries to attract humans,
Glowing with a flame of everlasting luminous orange.
Outlined with a dazzling silver border,
The flame starts to glow,
The wax starts to drip,
Gradually, slowly, melting down and down.
It is crackling,
It seems almost fearless with radiant beams of
Glistening light to brighten its surroundings.
It never realised that its life was hanging on by a thin thread.
        Waiting until . . . *Gone out!*

Gemma Adams (10)
Thames View Junior School

THE CANDLE

The candle is red, it didn't get fed.
Said the red candle
'Please don't blow me out
I don't want to die,
Oh please, oh please.'

I am alive hooray, hooray,
I am happy hooray, hooray,
I don't want to die hooray, hooray,
I'm going to survive hooray, hooray,
If someone blows me out
I will be dead.

Hannah Botting (10)
Thames View Junior School

THE RAIN

The rain is falling like a baby's tear,
It falls onto the window but the rain is clear.
It's as clear as the water out of the tap,
When it hits the window it's nice and flat,
As flat as a pancake on its back.
The rain is howling in the sky
Like a person's heart breaking,
Then a cry.
The rain is settling,
Now the sky is clear,
It will come back tomorrow
Like that baby's tear.

Lisa Large (11)
Thames View Junior School

MY CAT

C andy is my cat
A nd she likes to watch TV
N ibbles at her biscuits
D ives on her toys
Y ou would think she's funny

M y little sister
Y ou would love her

C os she's my cuddly cat
A nd she's all I ever want
T ime for bed, sweet dreams Candy.

Nicola Palfreyman (10)
Thames View Junior School

FIREWORKS

I saw a firework in the sky,
I saw a traffic light zooming by.
I saw a Catherine wheel twirling around
And when it finished it crashed to the ground.
I remember the loud bang at the end,
I could see the colours starting to bend.
A sparkler sparkles through the night
And don't forget to hold it tight.
We can't forget the golden rain,
Just make sure it does not fall down the drain.
We sing songs around the blazing fire,
To wait until the flames grow higher.

Siân Dane (10)
Thames View Junior School

MUM VS BOY

Go upstairs *now*
No, I'm finishing supper
When I say *now* I mean *now*
Shadupp, ya stupid sucker.

Why you liddle
You moron
You should be crying in your room.

I'm not crying
I'm not up
So why don't you lot
Just shaddup.

Glenn Buck (9)
Thames View Junior School

CANDLE

I'm shut inside a cupboard
I'm all alone
Nobody to talk to
Nothing to do
But once every year
I come out
Someone comes to light me
To me it's just the same
The flame comes towards me
Hotter and hotter
And gently place the flame on top of me
I feel so embarrassed
Everyone looking at me
As I slowly burn out.

Jane Cook (10)
Thames View Junior School

SAD CANDLE

It's flickering brightly side to side,
A touch of white
Glimmering quite.
The way it turns,
Sad, alone,
It would be cosy to have your own.
Burning, turning,
The lovely smell of smoke.
It can't get a chance to say
What it wants to say,
Because it's just a bright
Shiny flame.

Jade Kent (10)
Thames View Junior School

A CANDLE

Standing tall, all alone,
Waving, dancing up and down,
Slowly burning away.
Shimmering in the wind,
It is melting as it burns.
Glowing yellow,
The candle's happy.
The candle's sad,
Burning fast.
Slowly and sadly,
It burns away.
No more candle
Until next year.

Lauren Hyatt-Green (9)
Thames View Junior School

CANDLE

Lonely, sitting on the chair,
Makes everybody want to stare,
Quivering over there.
Makes everybody over there want to stare,
Sad but bright over there,
Lonely sitting on the chair.

Quietly melting over there,
Lonely sitting on the chair,
Red and twinkling over there.
Lonely sitting on the chair,
Glimmering, waving over there,
Lonely sitting on the chair.

Chloe Pemble (9)
Thames View Junior School

YOUNG IS JUST MEMORY

Young is just a memory from 6 years ago.
I used to wear a red ribbon with a little bow.
I used to climb on the beds and play with my sledge.
I used to wear a little pinafore but now I'm in class 4.
I could have cried more than once a day,
But I used to get tough with each day.
I would not get it in my sighs!
But I could not say my goodbyes.

Young is just a memory from 6 years ago.
I used to wear a red ribbon with a little bow.
No point in playing I-spy
As I've learnt to say a goodbye.

Charlotte Biddle (9)
Thames View Junior School

WHAT HAPPENED IN MY LIFE

When I was one it wasn't that much fun,
When I was two I could walk and talk,
When I was three I gulped down a bun,
When I was four I could talk aloud,
When I was five I went to school,
When I was six I wasn't that clever,
When I was seven I had a pool,
When I was eight I was very very clever.

Michael O'Neill (8)
Thames View Junior School

THE STORM

The storm flies swiftly through the sky.
I can hear it, it is flying this way.
The crying wind runs through my window.
Then the thunder crashes with an orchestra.
Then the lightning flashes and runs away again.
The storm then passes by and goes away
To destroy another village, another day.

Cara Nicholson (11)
Thames View Junior School

THE SMELLY SMOKY CANDLE

The smelly smoky candle,
Flashes side to side,
First still, then to a side.
The flame frantically flashing side to side,
Up and down,
And it stays there all alone
Melting and thinking what it was made from.

Jack Bulmer (9)
Thames View Junior School

THE CANDLES

They light up the house
when the electric goes
the flame goes up high
and burns down the candle
they come in different colours
red, yellow, blue and pink.

Michaela Veares (9)
Thames View Junior School

DARKNESS

Shadows are climbing over me.
I can hear the faint rustling in the bushes.
The squealing bats.
The homeless dogs and cats.
I'm scared.
The moon is gleaming and sparkling.
The odd shapes in the sky.

Lee Grainger (11)
Thames View Junior School

FLOWER

Flower, flower
Come back soon,
In the springtime afternoon.
It grows and grows until it's big,
It opens up its petals
To look up at the sun.

Katie Barron (10)
Thames View Junior School

THE SANDSTORM

The sand charges at me like a bullet out of a gun,
The sand is on the run,
It isn't much fun.
The wind is so strong, it sweeps the sand high,
Right up into the sky,
As though it can fly,
Like a butterfly.

Richard Edwards (10)
Thames View Junior School

CANDLES

Candles shimmer, shine, shake,
They dance and quiver,
The cheerful smoke going up,
Misty appearance blurred and hazy,
Waxy stick and flickering flame.

Amelia Heather (10)
Thames View Junior School

CANDLE

The candle is always complaining
It burns too hot for itself
But when put out it is too cold
The candle you cannot please
The candle is always complaining.

Nathan Robinson (9)
Thames View Junior School

THE FIREWORK DISPLAY

In your pocket never put a rocket
Because it will pull your arm from its socket.
Never put it in your hand because it is banned,
Enjoy the display but keep well away.
Just think hospital is not a very good holiday.

Sean Cackett (10)
Thames View Junior School

AUTUMN

Autumn is cold, crispy and silent,
Orange, yellow and red, leaves fall down,
Spinning around as they fall to the ground,
I like autumn, damp and wet.

Katy Webber (8)
Thames View Junior School

DAWN RAID

Machine guns chattered,
Rifles cracked,
Many were slain
But on and on they came.

Pistols spat,
Grenades roared,
Many were slain
But on and on they came.

The dirty troops exuded sweat,
Fixing bayonets and checking the parapet
As on and on they came.

Combat raged
With clash of steel
As men fought with determined zeal.

We pushed them back,
We forced them back,
Back from whence they came.

Edward Buggé (11)
Wellesley House School

THE KILLER SHEEP

For Christmas I was given a bike,
So, tired of walking, I thought I'd like
To feed my sheep by riding there.
I felt the wind against my hair
As I raced along the winding road,
Doing tricks as I'd been showed,
Until I reached my darling sheep.
The slope on the hill was very steep
So I usually stood clear from the edge
But today with inexplicable courage
I crept a little closer to admire
The magnificent view of our church spire.
The sheep were bleating like mad
As usual, for they were quite glad
To see the one who brings them stuff
To eat; then one tugged my cuff.
I turned around and there they were:
Muffin, Nina, Nani and Spur,
All pushing and tugging at me.
Then one rammed its head into my knee,
I swayed and fell right off the edge,
Luckily, I landed in a soft hedge
But then I saw my bike come after,
Gaining in speed, getting faster and faster.
There was no time for moving
And then came the very
Unsoothing thought of *death*.

Laura Sarao (11)
Wellesley House School

THE SEA BASS

I'm a large sea bass, not a herring or a crab,
But I'm still lying here on the fishmonger's slab.
It doesn't seem natural, it doesn't seem fair
For a fish like me to be breathing fresh air.
There's a woman in the shop looking strangely at me
As I've just heard her say I'm as fresh as can be.
I don't like the way that they're sharpening that knife,
It seems I'll be lucky to escape with my life.
What's that odd smell? I don't like that!
Oh no, oh no! They're heating the fat!
I'd better be quick if I'm to get out of here
Or they'll probably poach me in parsley and beer.
I'll gather my strength now and take a great leap,
(My appointment with Chef I am not going to keep.)
Goodbye foul restaurant, goodbye smelly shop!
I'll jump from the table and then off I'll hop,
For a fish like me should be swimming in water,
Minding my business and doing what I oughter.

Kiri Barker (11)
Wellesley House School

THOUGHTS OF DEATH

She has lost her shining light,
That which once had shone so bright,
Dying like a burning flame,
Her heart might never beat again.
Was she going to leave us here
With thoughts of death and those of fear?
Or was she going to live and stay
And try to find a different way -
A different way to mend her wrongs
And write more rules and sing more songs?
Was this to be her last long breath
That commits her to a lonely death,
Then place our thoughts into His hand
That guides her to an unknown land.

Rosanna Tennant (11)
Wellesley House School

JUST A WARNING

Not far away stands a proud, stubborn mountain,
With a proud, stubborn dragon sleeping inside it,
And I've heard that the mountain has many a secret,
And one, oh . . . he'd die upon fire to hide it.

Many a curious youth went and sought it,
You'd think that they never ever returned.
But they came back as dragons, and killed most the people,
Just because, wretched dragons, their stomachs churned.

The fiends took off and flew from their poor, wasted victims,
Even children suffered from being savagely beaten.
All the animals had been skewered and taken away,
And yet more people died, for their food had been eaten.

Years later, a soldier rode up to the mountain,
This time, with the advantage of distance; a gun.
So he shot him while he was peacefully dozing,
And brought the good news to everyone.

But although he was dead, to all their delight,
And had been stuffed and mounted like an unfortunate bear,
The same dragon's been spotted, back in the cave!
I can just hear him roar from his dark rocky lair . . .

So, I know it is tempting, but heaven forbid,
That another should seek him . . . they shan't even try!
You know you can't stop him, so please spread the word,
Dogs are one thing, but let sleeping dragons lie.

Meryl Trussler (10)